FOREWORD

This publication has been prepared under our direction for use by our respective commands and other commands as appropriate.

WILLIAM W. HARTZOG
General, USA
Commander
Training and Doctrine Command

J. E. RHODES
Lieutenant General, USMC
Commanding General
Marine Corps Combat
    Development Command

B. J. SMITH
Rear Admiral, USN
Commander
Navy Warfare Development Command

RONALD E. KEYS
Major General, USAF
Commander
Headquarters Air Force Doctrine Center

This publication is available on the Army Doctrinal and Training Digital Library (ADTDL) at http: //155.217.58.58

PREFACE

1. Scope

This multiservice procedures publication acts as a ready reference source for guidance on air traffic control (ATC) responsibilities, procedures, and employment in a joint environment. It discusses joint air traffic control (JATC) employment and Service relationships for initial, transition, and sustained ATC operations across the spectrum of joint operations within the theater or area of responsibility (AOR). This publication is UNCLASSIFIED and specifically addresses Service ATC doctrine, forces, capabilities, equipment, and training.

2. Purpose

This JATC publication meets the needs of the Services by providing procedures on JATC employment and by detailing Service relationships for initial, transition, and sustained JATC operations within the theater or AOR. It also outlines how to synchronize and integrate JATC forces and specialized ATC equipment.

3. Application

This publication applies to the operating forces of all Services. Although the focus of the publication is at the tactical level, it has application for planning and warfighting personnel at all levels. The target audience for this publication includes commanders, staffs, and agencies at all levels within and supporting a joint force.

4. Implementation Plan

Participating Service command offices of primary responsibility (OPRs) will review this publication, validate the information, and reference and incorporate it in Service manuals, regulations, and curricula as follows:

Army. The Army will incorporate the procedures in this publication in United States (US) Army training and doctrinal publications as directed by the commander, US Army Training and Doctrine Command (TRADOC). Distribution is in accordance with DA Form 12-99-R.

Marine Corps. The Marine Corps will incorporate the procedures in this publication in US Marine Corps training and doctrinal publications as directed by the commanding general, US Marine Corps Combat Development Command (MCCDC). Distribution is in accordance with MCPDS.

Navy. The Navy will incorporate these procedures in US Navy training and doctrinal publications as directed by the commander, Navy Warfare Development Command (NWDC). Distribution is in accordance with MILSTRIP Desk Guide and NAVSOP Publication 409.

Air Force. Air Force units will validate and incorporate appropriate procedures in accordance with applicable governing directives. Distribution is in accordance with AFI 37-160.

5. User Information

a. The TRADOC-MCCDC-NWDC-AFDC Air Land Sea Application (ALSA) Center developed this publication with the joint participation of the approving Service commands. ALSA will review and update this publication as necessary.

b. This publication reflects current joint and Service doctrine, command and control (C2) organizations, facilities, personnel, responsibilities, and procedures. Changes in Service protocol, appropriately reflected in joint and Service publications, will likewise be incorporated in revisions to this document.

c. We encourage recommended changes for improving this publication. Key your comments to the specific page and paragraph and provide a rationale for each recommendation. Send comments and recommendation directly to—

FM 100-104
MCRP 3-25A
NWP 3-56.3
AFTTP(I) 3-2.23

FM 100-104   US Army Training and Doctrine Command
                                          Fort Monroe, Virginia

MCRP 3-25A   Marine Corps Combat Development Command
                                          Quantico, Virginia

NWP 3-56.3   Navy Warfare Development Command
                                          Newport, Rhode Island

AFTTP(I) 3-2.23   Headquarters Air Force Doctrine Center
                                          Maxwell Air Force Base, Alabama

25 January 1999

JATC

Multiservice Procedures for Joint Air Traffic Control

TABLE OF CONTENTS

EXECUTIVE SUMMARY

JATC

Multiservice Procedures for Joint Air Traffic Control

Overview

This publication—

•Provides basic background information on JATC operations.

•Describes each Service's ATC doctrine, forces, capabilities, training, and equipment used to perform JATC operations.

•Outlines the duties, responsibilities, and command and control relationships that influence JATC operations and handover procedures.

•Illustrates how Service ATC forces are deployed and employed to perform ATC operations.

•Describes how Service ATC forces conduct ATC during initial, transition, and sustained operations.

•Outlines the process for synchronizing and integrating JATC forces within the theater or AOR.

•Explains how to integrate the Services' ATC equipment and ATC forces.

Doctrine, Forces, Capabilities, Equipment, and Training

Chapter I provides details on the four Services' ATC doctrine, forces, capabilities, training, and equipment. It provides a baseline understanding of component capabilities for conducting ATC operations in a joint environment by providing a description of—

• The doctrinal framework each Service uses to execute JATC operations.

• The Service-specific ATC forces capable of deploying and executing JATC operations.

• The Service-specific equipment and systems used to control air traffic in the theater or AOR.

• The specific ATC capabilities each Service has available.

• The training each Service provides for ATC personnel.

Operations and Procedures

Chapter II describes JATC operations and procedures. It outlines the duties, responsibilities, communications, and command and control relationships that influence ATC operations and handover procedures. It illustrates how ATC forces are deployed and employed to perform JATC operations. This chapter also provides a general description of how ATC forces conduct ATC during initial, transition, and sustained operations.

Planning Considerations for Initial, Transition, and Sustained JATC Operations

Chapter III explains how to integrate Services' ATC equipment and uniquely trained ATC forces. It also outlines a process for synchronization and integration of ATC forces within the theater or AOR. It provides ATC-specific checklists and considerations for joint planners.

INTRODUCTION

Although basic ATC operations throughout the Services share many commonalities, Service-unique requirements can cause operational problems if not anticipated. Improvements in JATC operations can be made by ensuring interoperable equipment; commonly accepted tactics, techniques, and procedures (TTP); and application of the TTP during development of joint and multiservice doctrine, joint training, exercises, and operations.

Current Service doctrine, as well as Joint Vision 2010, asserts that operating jointly is imperative for success. To accomplish this, aviation related elements of each Service must become thoroughly familiar with the organization, capabilities, and TTP of their own Service and those of each force-providing Service or nation.

This publication provides the Service-unique information a planner requires to employ ATC services in a joint environment. Included are suggested handover considerations and checklists for use in joint planning and execution of ATC services in the progression of initial, transition, and sustained operations. A void seems to exist from the mission conclusion of special tactics (ST) forces combat controllers to the introduction of robust sustainment forces. Ways to employ appropriately equipped transition forces and a plan for timely relief of ST forces are addressed as well as the organizational and command structure differences that contribute to deployment and handover problems.

In all Services there is a lack of guidance for the transition of ATC operations from one Service to another. The only guidance provided suggests each Service consider the coordination and integration of air traffic services within their branch. In short, there are no TTP to plan the actual handover. This publication provides the TTP necessary to facilitate viable multiservice ATC operations until joint doctrine fully evolves to support JATC operations.

PROGRAM PARTICIPANTS

The following commands and agencies participated in the development of this publication:

Joint

Mobility Concepts Agency, Ft Monroe, VA
Joint Warfighting Center, Ft Monroe, VA
United States Southern Command, SCJ5-PS, Miami, FL
United States European Command, ECJ5, APO AE 09128
United States Pacific Command, J383, Camp H. M. Smith, HI
United States Transportation Command, TCJ5-SR, Scott AFB, IL
United States Space Command, SPJ5X, Peterson AFB, CO
North American Aerospace Defense Command, J-3, Peterson AFB, CO

Army

US Army Training and Doctrine Command, DCSDOC (ATDO-A), Ft Monroe, VA
US Army Aeronautical Services Agency, Ft Belvoir, VA
US Army Command and General Staff College, Ft Leavenworth, KS
29th Air Traffic Services Group, Aberdeen Proving Ground, MD
US Army DCSOPS Aviation, Washington DC
US Army Air Traffic Control Activity (ATZQ-ATC), Ft Rucker, AL
1-58 Aviation Regiment (ATC), Ft Bragg, NC
18th Aviation Brigade, Ft Bragg, NC

Marine Corps

Marine Corps Combat Development Command, Joint Doctrine Br (C427), Quantico, VA
Marine Aviation Weapons and Tactics Squadron 1, Yuma, AZ

Navy

Commander, Naval Doctrine Command, Norfolk Naval Base, Norfolk, VA
COMTACGRU-2, NAB Little Creek, Norfolk, VA

Air Force

Headquarters Air Force Doctrine Center, Det 1, Langley AFB, VA
Headquarters Air Combat Command (SCX), Langley AFB, VA
Headquarters Air Combat Command (DOF), Langley AFB, VA
Headquarters Air Force Special Operations Command (DOOF), Hurlburt Field, FL
Headquarters Air Force Special Operations Command (XPP), Hurlburt Filed, FL
Headquarters Air Mobility Command (DOA), Scott AFB, IL
Headquarters United States Air Force (XOOS), Washington DC
720th Special Tactics Group, Hurlburt Filed, FL
OLA, 720th Special Tactics Group, Scott AFB, IL
24th Special Tactics Squadron, Pope AFB, NC
609th Combat Plans Squadron, Shaw AFB, SC
Air Force Flight Standards Agency, Andrews AFB, MD
Aerospace Command and Control Agency, Langley AFB, VA

Air National Guard

Headquarters Air National Guard (XOB), Washington, DC

Chapter I

DOCTRINE, FORCES, CAPABILITIES, EQUIPMENT, AND TRAINING

1. Background

Each Service maintains its own air traffic control (ATC) schools, which provide duplication of initial ATC training. Each trains to Federal Aviation Administration (FAA) standards and produces knowledgeable, technically competent graduates capable of transitioning from apprentice to full-performance level air traffic controllers. These basic skills are then honed to a higher level, consistent with the level of air traffic serviced. All Service controllers start out with the same basic skills, but unique mission requirements dictate the experience level and special skills that are developed to meet mission requirements. Although each Service's advanced and sustainment ATC training and professional development is different, they meet the peacetime focus to develop the go-to-war skills required to support combat operations. This chapter details the ATC capabilities of all four Services including a snapshot of their doctrine, forces, capabilities, equipment, and training.

2. Army

a. Doctrine.

Army air traffic services (ATSs) are an extremely important function in the synchronization of combat power. ATS tactical units function as an integral element of joint, multinational, and interagency forces. These units must conduct both opposed and unopposed early entry operations. As a tailored force, ATS supports the Army during all phases of operations.

ATSs are integrated with the theater airspace management structure. Army ATS tactical units support joint operations at all echelons within the theater and operate independently of aviation brigades. ATS groups are in general support (GS) to a theater; ATS battalions and/or ATS companies are in GS to a corps. ATS companies are in direct support (DS) to a division and/or GS to a corps. See Appendix D.

(1) ATS Tactical Units.

ATS tactical units augment the operations (G-3 and J-3) of the field Army and land component commander with Army airspace command and control (A2C2) liaisons and airspace information center (AIC) services. The units augment at echelons above corps (EAC), corps, and division, including the aviation brigade if resources are available. These A2C2 cells provide multinational or interagency interface for ATS systems throughout the theater of operations. As part of the A2C2 element, the ATS support is the Army's primary coordination link to the Theater Air Ground System (TAGS).

ATS tactical units must coordinate airspace requirements, provide an interface for airspace coordination during execution, and provide an instrument recovery capability. A2C2 elements enhance force protection by relaying real-time situational awareness, deconfliction of airspace, synchronization, and integration of combat power. This information is critical to the survival of all airspace users. ATS tactical units perform airspace control functions based on the airspace control order (ACO) and the airspace control plan (ACP). The ACO and the ACP outline approved airspace control measures and other active airspace control procedures. The airspace control authority (ACA) publishes ACOs after approval by the joint force commander (JFC). ATS A2C2 personnel coordinate airspace control measures, control functions, and special procedures at all echelons to provide commanders maximum flexibility while conducting operations. The ACA is responsible for developing, coordinating, and publishing airspace control procedures in the area of responsibility (AOR)/joint operations area (JOA). Once airspace control measures and parameters have been approved, ATS elements operate in compliance with this guidance. Therefore, liaison between the ACA, ATS command and control (C2) structure, and other elements of the airspace control system (ACS) in theater is necessary to ensure that airspace control procedures are integrated and synchronized with Army forces (ARFOR) commander's requirements.

(2) Military Operations Other Than War (MOOTW). In MOOTW, the JFC's concept of operations often requires close liaison and coordination with the host nation's air traffic facilities and ACA (if it is separate). This is normally facilitated through the United States (US) ambassador's country team. ATS commanders and their liaison elements must be involved from the outset in the planning and execution of airspace and ATC. They ensure that airspace requirements supporting ATS operations are coordinated with and approved by the proper agency. These units may participate in the development of a host nation airspace infrastructure. This may involve training host nation ATS personnel or aviators in ATS operations and procedures. ATS personnel may provide planning, terminal airspace information, and forward-area support services to aviation assets conducting nation assistance.

b. Forces.

The deployment of ATS tactical units in a theater of operations depends on the extent ARFOR are committed. ATS tactical units and their organic teams are task organized to provide DS and GS to the ARFOR commander. They can also be task organized to support aviation operations as part of a separate joint task force (JTF). See Appendix A for more information.

c. Capabilities.

Army ATS tactical units have C2 responsibilities that provide forces with real-time airspace information and enhance synchronization of combat power. ATSs at all levels assist the A2C2 elements in integrating airspace requirements in the combined, joint, and/or interagency environment. (*Note: If resourced, A2C2 liaison support can be provided to division level aviation brigades.*) ATS capabilities include—effective ATS liaison, mobile ATS facilities, reliable communications, timely relay of intelligence, airspace coordination, and relay of accurate weather information.

ATS terminal facilities provide EAC, corps, and division with a ground controlled approach (GCA), instrument flight rules (IFR) airfield capability. Once established, these GCA approaches must meet terminal instrument procedures (TERPS) criteria in accordance with (IAW) *United States Standard Flight Inspection Manual* (TM 95-225, NAVAIR 16-1-520, AFM 11-225, FAA08200.1A) and *Terminal Instrument Procedures Manual* (TM 95-226, OPNAVINST 3722.16C, AFM 11-226, CG 318, FAAH 8260.3B). The approaches must also be flight checked by FAA certified personnel and equipment to become a certified instrument approach for any airspace user. AICs provide airspace guidance and an airspace management interface. ATS commanders and their staffs operating with liaison elements in tactical operations centers collect, process, display, issue, and coordinate critical C2 information. ATS terminal operations include a full range of ATC services (for helicopter and limited fixed-wing aircraft) to regulate landings and takeoffs, especially in areas of high-density traffic.

Upon completion of military objectives, ATS units are often required to support airspace and air traffic requirements during the post hostilities phase of operations. This support will normally remain in theater while US Army aviation assets are deployed or until allied or host nation ATS capabilities are adequate, sufficient, and proficient enough to support the JFC's requirements.

(1) Deep Operations. Tactical aviation control teams (TACTs) conduct ATS terminal operations in the deep operations area. Using lightweight, portable equipment, these teams can deploy with airborne, special operations forces (SOF), and long range surveillance (LRS) units to provide navigational assistance to aircraft during deep operations. In the deep battle area, ATS terminal operations include—providing weather and A2C2 information; conducting visual surveillance of austere drop zones (DZs), pick up zones (PZs), landing zones (LZs) and airheads; providing aviation advisories as required; and providing austere DZs, PZs, LZs, and airheads with on-call nonprecision approach navigational aids (NAVAIDS). See Appendix B.

(2) Close Operations. During close operations, ATS terminal operations will be limited. As required by the tactical situation, these operations will be set up in areas designated for priority logistics and medical evacuation. They will also be set up in forward arming and refueling points (FARPs) and maneuver force assembly areas. During close operations, ATS terminal operations include—providing A2C2 situational update information; providing visual surveillance of landing areas; providing aviation separation and sequencing of arriving and departing aircraft; providing NAVAIDS for nonprecision approaches for instrument meteorological conditions (IMC) recovery; providing short notice backup support if the battle tempo or the requirements to aid in resupply and reconstitution change;

providing positive or procedural control measures as required by environmental factors, the density and complexity of air traffic, and the airspace situation; and coordinating the movement of air traffic with other ATS facilities, A2C2 elements, and joint/multinational elements to effect an unimpeded flow of aircraft into and out of the close-battle area. This support is facilitated by direct liaison augmentation to the A2C2 architecture.

(3) Rear Operations.

ATS terminal operations in the rear are more robust than in the forward areas and provide established airfields, satellite/recovery airfields and all-weather capable landing areas in the theater, corps, and division AORs. Terminal operations include—efficient movement of aircraft, providing visual and electronic surveillance, providing traffic pattern separation and sequencing, providing precision or nonprecision approach NAVAIDS, and designing terminal area precision and nonprecision approaches. ATS airspace information centers supporting rear operations provide on-call demand activated en route NAVAIDS, dissemination of weather and critical flight data, en route aircraft separation and deconfliction on designated flight routes, interface with the other joint/multinational, interagency, and host nation airspace management systems, and a transition to the comprehensive en route airway structure used to support air traffic to and from the rear operations area.

When deployed as part of the initial entry forces, in combat operations or MOOTW, ATS tactical units will establish terminal operations at landing areas/sites as required. ATS tactical units provide—

(a) AIC. Airspace information services will be provided by the AIC as a secondary mission. AICs will provide a real-time air picture and communications with A2C2 staff elements and other ATS facilities and—

•Act as the executors of A2C2 elements by providing a real-time interface with A2C2 elements and airborne elements of the TAGS.

•Maintain secure and redundant communications/data links with ATS facilities, air defense facilities, and other elements of the ACS, TACT, and all manned users of assigned airspace and controlling elements of unmanned aerial vehicles (UAV). These services will link the user (the supported unit) and organic C2 network through secure communications.

•Provide the full range of airspace user information and weather information (obscuring phenomena, extreme weather, pilot reports).

•Move with the maneuver/ supported forces, while simultaneously providing a communication link with airspace C2 system users.

•Provide navigational assistance while managing operations within the preplanned en route structure.

•Coordinate en route traffic with TACTs and terminal facilities (airfields/ landing areas).

•Provide deconfliction, synchronization, and airspace user separation throughout the supported commander's battlespace as necessary.

•Coordinate movements to and from rapid refueling points (RRPs)/FARPs.

•Maintain locations and status of RRPs/FARPs, terminal facilities, and NAVAIDS.

•Provide assistance for instrument or maintenance recovery of aircraft in distress/emergency.

•Provide a backup C2 link for operational commanders.

•Provide flight following for any manned airspace user and situational awareness of UAVs.

•Assist in combat search and rescue (CSAR) missions.

(b) Terminal Services. ATS personnel and equipment perform services/ functions that facilitate movement, takeoff, and landing of aircraft to/from a particular point/place on the ground (landing area), regardless of weather conditions. The amount and type of terminal service support is mission, enemy, terrain and weather, troops and support available, time available (METT-T) dependent. Terminal service personnel and equipment are mobile, deployable, possess night vision devices (NVDs), compatible with day/night signaling devices, and are capable of providing—

•Terminal services to a full spectrum of rotary aircraft and limited services for fixed-wing aircraft; terminal services can also provide fully instrumented precision approach/ sequencing capability, tower, operations, and crash/rescue operations to temporary, austere, hastily prepared landing strips/ areas. These services can be performed from captured enemy facilities (airheads), existing host nation facilities, or engineer prepared facilities.

•Airfield management support at EAC and division, as required (for example, airfield operations and airfield commanders supported by crash rescue).

•ATS terminal facilities with the organic capability to provide mobile, light, ground to air communications, tactical lighting for rotary-wing LZ/PZ, weather dissemination, and limited NAVAIDS support at selected landing areas.

•Arrival, departure, and special information during all-weather conditions on a 24-hour basis.

•Precision and/or nonprecision NAVAIDS for IMC recovery.

•Sequencing and separation of aircraft at designated landing areas.

•Input to the airspace procedures guide (APG) after coordination with supported users.

(c) Forward Area Support Services/TACTs. TACTs provide pathfinder/air assault capabilities to all airspace users operating in support of predominantly deep and close operations. They will be capable of supporting LZ, PZ, FARP, DZ, airhead, laager, and other similar type operations. They will be linked with the overall A2C2/ATS support system through organic voice and data communications. Additionally, they possess some of the same capabilities as the terminal service. TACTs also possess and provide—

•24-hour support for tactical and/or peacetime operations through the use of portable long range, secure, jam resistant, data burst communication packages, global positioning system (GPS), and NVDs.

•Mobile, highly deployable teams with pathfinder capabilities; teams require minimal logistical support, but their tactical movement is dependent upon the mobility of the supported unit.

•Immediate support in response to an ever changing, fluid battle field.

•Long range nonline of sight (NLOS), secure, and antijam communications capability (voice and data), normally operating in the deep battle area cross forward line of own troops (X-FLOT) and close battle area supporting combat operations (that is, communicating with airspace users and parent air intercept controller).

•Movement into and out of unimproved and austere landing areas to include PZs, DZs, FARPs/RRPs, and airheads.

•Force packaged and task organized, capable of performing operations at multiple locations simultaneously.

•Extended secure communications capabilities of the AICs and forward deployed C2 elements and current information about the air activity in and around TACTs areas of operations.

•Portable NAVAIDS for pre-planned and on-call missions, for example, approach aids (includes visual multi-spectral NAVAIDS), identification and manning passage points, FARPs/RRPs landing sites, navigational update points/fixes, and other missions as required by the maneuver or aviation commander.

•Near real-time information to supported elements/commanders command, control, communication, and intelligence (C3I) networks directly and through the TACT's electronic link with the AICs.

•Meteorological/situational updates and interface with joint and host nation forces operating in the same area of operations.

•Contingency or backup elements capable of performing terminal and en route functions.

(d) A2C2 Services.

•General. A2C2 provides a three dimensional data handling/display capability (computer and software) to provide ATS A2C2 elements at all echelons, division and above (at the aviation brigades if resources are available), plus the situation awareness to quickly plan, coordinate, and deconflict airspace. A2C2 staff elements must also possess the capability to disseminate situational awareness information to other ATS elements and airspace users.

•Tactical. Army ATS tactical units must deploy early to enable JFCs to conduct force buildup operations and sustain early entry forces. These units are normally integrated into the first echelon of deploying forces and provide critical airspace management, C2, and terminal services to ensure mission success. ATS personnel must be manifested on the same sorties as other joint airspace planners (that is, air operations center [AOC], battlefield coordination detachment [BCD], and A2C2 elements) with which they habitually operate. This allows Army aviation operational requirements to be fully integrated into the joint force operations airspace requirements. Early employment of ATS personnel and equipment lays the foundation for effective arrival and deployment of transition forces.

d. Equipment.

(1) Current Systems. Army ATC equipment and systems are designed to support the JFC's airspace and air traffic needs. Appendix E contains a description of the most current and the anticipated US Army air traffic equipment and systems. Current ATS systems include—

(a) AN/TSW-7A, ATC Central—provides control tower operations for transition and sustained ATS operations.

(b) AN/TSC-61B, Flight Coordination Center (FCC)—provides procedural flight following and airspace coordination for transition and sustained ATS operations.

(c) AN/TSQ-71B, (TPN-18) Landing Control Central—provides precision approach radar services and limited surveillance radar services for transition and sustained ATS operations.

(d) AN/TSQ-97 and AN/TSQ-198, ATC Facility—provides visual flight rules (VFR) tower services for initial ATS operations.

(e) AN/TRN-30 (V) 1 and (V) 2, Radio Beacon Set—provides automatic direction finding (ADF) navigational aid for initial, transition and sustained ATS operations.

(2) Communications Equipment. ATS forces must communicate on the move and maintain and sustain the same communications capabilities as other maneuver forces. Throughout the range of military operations, ATS tactical units must be able to communicate with local airspace authorities and host nation airspace infrastructures using telephones and radios. Radio is the primary means of internal and external communications. ATS tactical units use frequency modulation (FM), high frequency (HF), amplitude modulation (AM) voice, very high frequency (VHF), ultra high frequency (UHF), common-user systems, and internal wire to expedite C2. The AIC requires access to satellite communications (SATCOM) intelligence and weather broadcasts. SATCOM also serves as the NLOS backup means of communications. ATS tactical units require dual HF for simultaneous voice and data transmission and reception.

e. Acquisition Programs. ATS tactical units will continue to employ en route and NAVAIDS until space-based systems can satisfy this requirement. Several modernization programs are underway to keep pace with requirements until this transition occurs. The following acquisition programs will greatly enhance ATS support in the future:

(1) AN/TSQ-198, Tactical Terminal Control System (TTCS)—(62 systems) for worldwide use in the production/deployment phase. The AN/TSQ-198 is a replacement for the current TSQ-97 and will address deficiencies in security and maintainability. This system is currently being fielded.

(2) Air Traffic Navigation, Integration, and Coordination System

(ATNAVICS)–(38 systems) for worldwide use. First Unit Equipped (FUE) fiscal year (FY) 00. ATNAVICS is a replacement for the AN/TSQ-71B and will provide a highly mobile surveillance and precision approach radar system that can be transported with its prime mover on a single C-130 and installed in 1 hour.

(3) Tactical Airspace Integration System (TAIS)–(52 systems) for worldwide use—currently in low rate initial production (LRIP). TAIS is a replacement for the AN/TSC-61B. TAIS will provide a fully automated capability in support of A2C2 and airspace information services (AIS). The TAIS is planned for employment in any theater of operations for any mission where the Army will execute A2C2 and/or ATS functions. Currently, the TAIS will be employed at EACs, corps, and division level. TAIS wartime responsibilities center on A2C2 planning and execution, battlespace synchronization, and ATS support. TAIS MOOTW functions center on the task force mission and include A2C2 planning and execution, expansion of regional civil or host nation ATS/ATC responsibilities, and/or government interagency operations.

(4) Mobile Tower System (MOTS)–(38 systems) for worldwide use. It replaces the AN/TSQ-70A and AN/TSW-7A. MOTS acquisition may be accelerated if the program is elevated via inclusion on Department of Defense (DOD) Rapid Acquisition Program. A decision is pending. For further discussion, refer to Appendices D and E.

f. Training. Initial training for Army air traffic controllers is conducted at Fort Rucker, Alabama. Upon completion of initial training, a graduate is qualified for worldwide assignment to a fixed base tower, GCA radar, or a tactical ATC unit. AR 611-201 covers the requirements and qualifications of individuals completing this training. See Appendix C.

(1) Fixed Base Ratings. There are five classifications of fixed Army ATC facilities: airfield/heliport ATC tower, GCA radar, Army flight following service, *Army approach control (nonradar), and *Army radar approach control. (*The Army has these types of facilities; however, no active duty Army personnel are assigned.)

(a) Fixed Facility Tower Rating. A fixed facility tower rating consists of the controller completing a facility orientation and rating program. The rating program requires a controller to complete 6 months of on-the-job training (OJT), the facility training program (FTP), limited weather observer certification, and an over-the-shoulder evaluation on all ATS facility positions, by an FAA Certified Training Operator (CTO)/Air Traffic Control Specialist Examiner. The certification is recorded on DA Form 3479-1-R. The FAA CTO/Air Traffic Control Specialist Examiner is designated IAW AR 95-2, FAA Order 7220.1, and FM 1-303. Evaluations are administered IAW FAR, Part 65, FAA Orders 7220.1 and 8080.1. Once the controller has satisfactorily completed this process, the rating will be annotated on both the FAA Certified Tower Operator Card and the FAA Form 7220-1 Air Traffic Control Specialist Card.

(b) Fixed GCA Rating. A fixed GCA rating consists of the controller completing a facility orientation and rating program. The rating program requires a controller to complete 4 months of OJT, the FTP, and an over-the-shoulder evaluation, on all ATS facility positions, by a FAA certified CTO/air traffic control specialist examiner and recorded on DA Form 3479-1-R. The FAA CTO/air traffic control specialist examiner is designated IAW AR 95-2, FAA Order 7220.1 and FM 1-303. Evaluations are administered IAW FAR, Part 65, FAA Orders 7220.1, and 8080.1. Once the controller has satisfactory completed this process the rating will be annotated on the FAA Form 7220-1 Air Traffic Control Specialist Card. It takes 6 to 8 months to train with the tactical GCA.

(c) Fixed Flight Following Facility Rating. A fixed flight following facility rating consists of the controller completing a facility orientation and rating program. The rating program requires a controller to complete 3 months of OJT, the FTP, and an over-the-shoulder evaluation on all ATS facility positions, by a FAA certified CTO/air traffic control specialist examiner and recorded on DA Form 3479-1-R. The FAA CTO/air traffic control specialist examiner is designated IAW AR 95-2, FAA Order 7220.1 and FM 1-303. Evaluations are administered IAW FAR, Part 65, FAA Orders 7220.1 and 8080.1. Once the controller has satisfactory completed this process the rating will be annotated on the FAA Form 7220-1 Air Traffic Control Specialist Card.

(2) Tactical Certification Program.

Tactical Army ATC facilities are grouped into three major classifications: ATC tower (tactical tower [tac twr] and TACT), GCA radar, and Army airspace information services/A2C2 liaison officer (LNO).

The Tactical Certification Program will consist of two phases, *Qualification* and *Rating*, IAW FM 1-303. Phase-I, *Qualification*, consists of tactical equipment knowledge. Phase-II, *Rating*, evaluates the controllers ability to control traffic in a tactical environment by applying standard ATS rules and procedures, to use standard phraseology, and to perform administrative duties in a tactical ATS facility.

Within 60 days of assignment to an ATS platoon, all controllers will be entered into a Tactical Certification Program. Additionally, controllers must complete the training program within 4 calendar months from the date of entry. All controllers entered into the Tactical Certification Program are required to be proficient on the installation, maintenance, and operation of all assigned tactical ATS and service support equipment associated with their unit's mission.

Platoon sergeants/section sergeants ensure that each controller presents the following documents to the examiner before entry into the certification program: Training and Proficiency Record-Air Traffic Controller, DA Form 3479-R, and FAA Form 7220.1 Air Traffic Control Specialist Certificate.

A written examination will be administered to effectively evaluate the trainees training and proficiency. The tactical examination will consist of a practical equipment knowledge evaluation (hands on evaluation) and an over-the-shoulder evaluation on all ATS facility positions, recorded on DA Form 3479-1-R. A FAA CTO/Air Traffic Control Specialist Examiner conducts the evaluations.

The FAA CTO/Air Traffic Control Specialist Examiner is designated IAW AR 95-2, FAA Order 7220.1, and FM 1-303. Evaluations are administered IAW FAR, Part 65, FAA Orders 7220.1 and 8080.1.

The A2C2 LNOs receive OJT at the division, corps, and EAC levels. The only current prerequisite to be assigned as an A2C2 LNO is the completion of the United States Air Force (USAF) Joint Firepower Command and Control Course at the Air Ground Operations School (AGOS), Nellis Air Force Base, Nevada.

3. Marine Corps

a. Doctrine/Organization.

The Marine Corps organizes its forces for employment by integrating four functional elements: ground combat, air combat, combat service support, and command into one cohesive task force, the Marine air-ground task force (MAGTF). A MAGTF can range in size from small special purpose units to large Marine expeditionary forces (MEFs). The MAGTF is organized to meet the continuing demands of modern combat by coordinating a diverse array of assets under the control of a single commander.

The aviation combat element (ACE) adds a unique capability and dimension to the MAGTF by dramatically increasing its firepower, mobility, and area of influence. This common theme links the six major functional responsibilities of Marine aviation and establishes the foundation for aviation support (see Figure I-1).

Marine ATC is a valuable asset in the forward operating base (FOB) concept for MAGTF aviation operations. Depending on the scope of MAGTF operations, it is often necessary to establish ATC service at a main air base, air facility, and air site but also at a FARP, rapid ground refueling (RGR) points, and laager points. The FOB concept typically requires mobile ATC capabilities.

b. Forces.

The employment of a MAGTF requires the close integration of air and ground force operations. The MAGTF commander employs the Marine Air Command and Control System (MACCS) to monitor, supervise, and influence ACE air operations. The MACCS is not a piece of hardware but rather an integrated group of C2 agencies. The MACCS provides the ACE commander with the air C2 support facilities and infrastructure necessary to command, coordinate, and control air operations within an assigned area of operation or airspace sector and to coordinate MAGTF air operations with other Services. Principal MACCS agencies are provided, operated, and maintained by a Marine air control group (MACG).

The Marine ATC detachment (MATCD) is the principal terminal ATC organization within the MACCS. Four MACTDs are structured to operate as subordinate elements of the Marine air control squadron (MACS). Figure I-2 depicts the MACG units and their respective agencies and detachments.

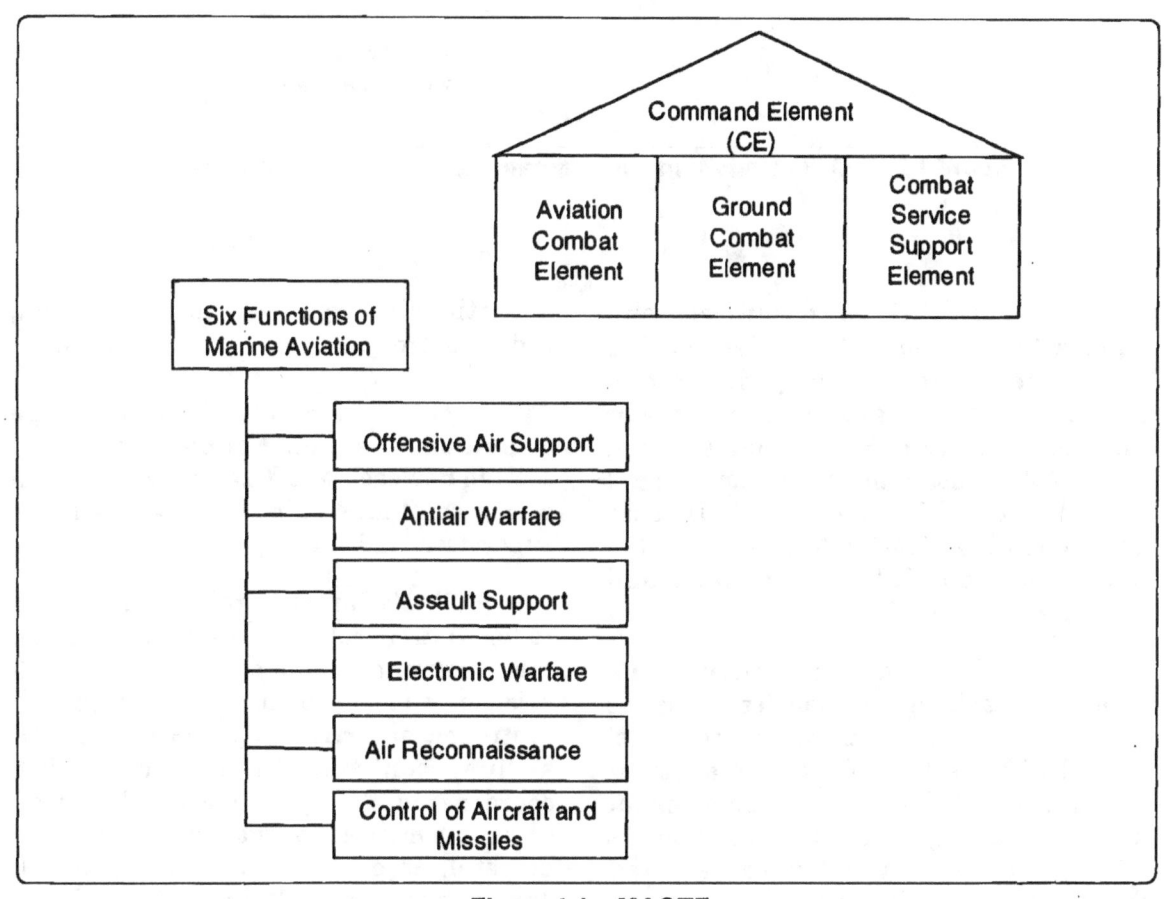

Figure I-1. MAGTF

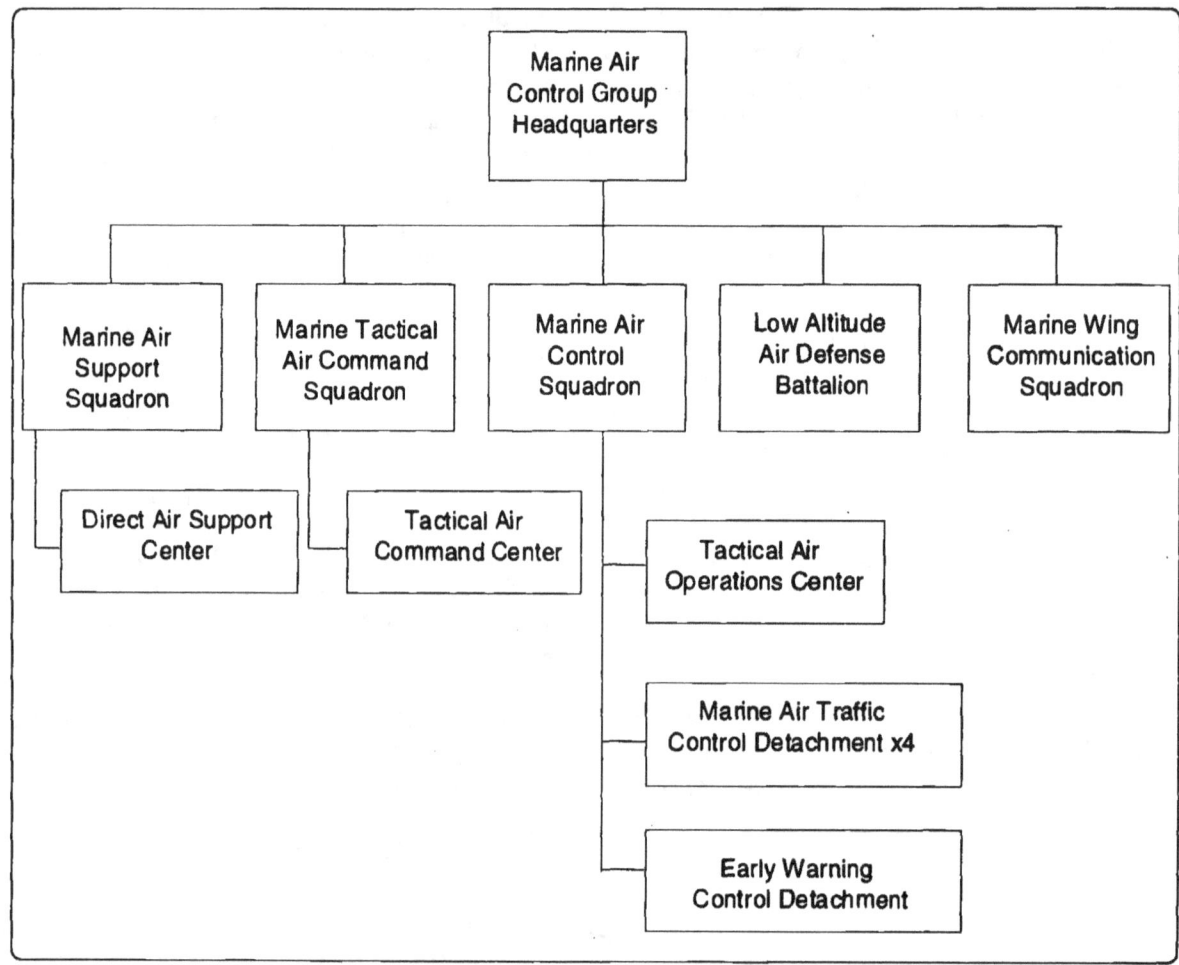

Figure I-2. MACG Units and Subordinate Agencies and Detachments

Each MATCD is organized and equipped to provide continuous all-weather ATC services to an independent and geographically separated main air base or air facility and/or remote air site or point. The MATCD also functions as an integral part of a MAGTF Integrated Air Defense System (IADS). Marine ATC equipment is maintained by MATCD personnel and supported by NAVAIR.

The MATCD's assigned mission and supporting task organization determine the ATC element's exact crew requirements. The MATCD is headed by a detachment commander who coordinates detachment activities and supervises the detachment's ATC watch officers. Watch officers are crew managers. MATCD crews are typically operationally organized into command, radar control, and tower control sections.

(1) Command Section. The command section supervises and coordinates each MATCD's activities. It is composed of an ATC watch officer, a radar supervisor, and a tower supervisor.

(2) Radar Control Section. The radar control section is responsible for the management of assigned/designated airspace and is composed of an approach controller, an arrival/departure controller, a final controller, and a data link coordinator. The radar control section transmits information via data link or voice crosstell to other air control agencies, supervises MATCD execution of the

emission control (EMCON) conditions set by the Marine tactical air command center (TACC), and employs electronic protection (EP) measures as appropriate.

(3) Control Section.

The control section is responsible for the control of friendly aircraft operating within the tower's assigned airspace. This airspace is typically limited to an area that can be visually observed and surveyed from the tower (approximately a 5-mile radius from the airport up to an altitude of 2500 feet above ground level). The tower control section is also responsible for air and vehicular traffic operating on runways, taxiways, and other designated areas of the airfield. The tower control section is composed of a local controller, ground controller, and a flight data operator.

Each detachment is organized to provide the MAGTF with one Marine ATC mobile team (MMT). The MMT is a task-organized subelement of the MATCD. Normally the lead element in establishing initial ATC service, the MMT is responsible for rapidly establishing and controlling tactical landing zones (TLZs) for fixed-wing aircraft and helicopter landing zones (HLZs) for rotary-wing and vertical/short takeoff and landing (V/STOL) aircraft in remote locations under both visual meteorological conditions (VMC) and IMC. MMTs typically deploy with a MEU. Figure I-3 depicts the crew structure for both the MATCD and MMT.

c. Capabilities (See Appendix B).

(1) Support Operations. The MATCD is capable of deploying and operating independent of the MAGTF, joint force, or JTF to provide ATC support for various types of operations. Examples of this type of ATC support include—

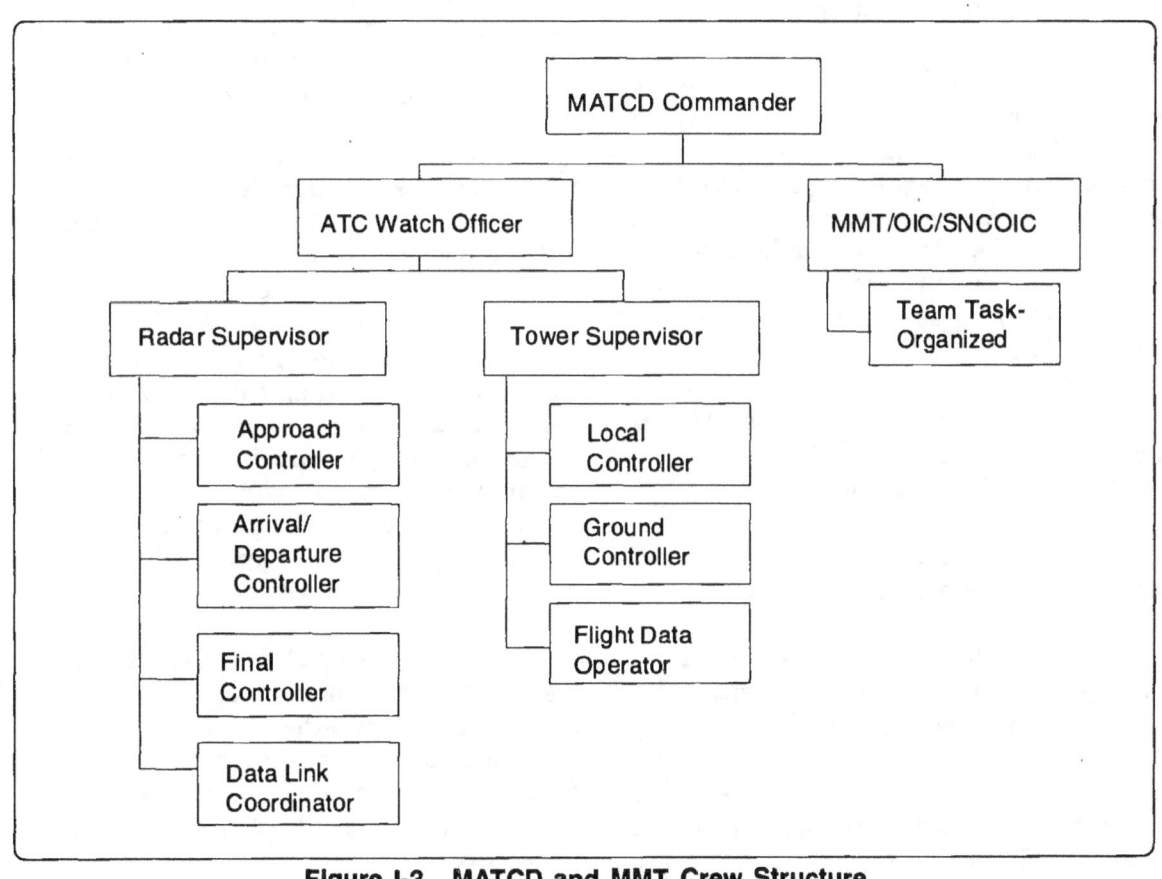

Figure I-3. MATCD and MMT Crew Structure

(a) Providing ATC service to assist humanitarian efforts (MOOTW).

(b) Assisting other joint/allied services.

(c) Supporting intergovernmental ATC requirements.

(2) Missions. The MATCD functions as an integral part of the MAGTF's airspace management and air defense networks. In the accomplishment of its mission, the MATCD—

(a) Provides control tower, radar, and nonradar approach/departure control services within its assigned airspace.

(b) Provides precision and nonprecision NAVAIDS.

(c) Provides automatic landing system approach and landing services under all-weather conditions.

(d) Displays and disseminates appropriate air and ground situation information to designated higher and adjacent air C2 agencies to include—Marine TACC, tactical air operations center (TAOC), direct air support center (DASC), and low altitude air defense units while functioning as an integral element of the MACCS.

(e) Serves as the operational liaison between the MAGTF and national/international ATC agencies.

(f) Coordinates the activation of the airfield base defense zone (BDZ).

(g) Provides airspace control, management, and surveillance within its designated airspace sector.

(h) Provides navigational assistance to friendly aircraft, to include itinerant ATC services.

(i) Interfaces with the MACCS, other military air control agencies, and/or civilian agencies/authorities, as necessary.

(j) Provides required ATC services in support of MAGTF operations.

(k) Provides personnel to the survey liaison reconnaissance party (SLRP) team to ensure MATCD siting criteria and TERPS are considered and addressed during the site survey.

(3) Employment Options.

The MATCD can be task organized to meet any number of different contingency operations. The ATC services required at a FOB will dictate the specific number of personnel and types of equipment necessary to support the mission. While a particular MATCD configuration may normally be associated with a MEF, special purpose MAGTF (SPMAGTF), or MEU, the specific requirements for a given tactical situation will dictate the actual configuration suitable for mission success.

Each MATCD is capable of providing the full range of terminal ATC services. Primary employment options may include, but are not limited to—

(a) Full Service ATCD. This detachment is designed to support continuous all-weather ATC services at a main air base. Services provided by these detachments typically include—control tower, tactical air navigation (TACAN), radar approach, and arrival/departure control, precision/nonprecision, and instrument approaches.

(b) Tower and TACAN Detachment. This detachment's capabilities focus on providing all-weather ATC services at a designated site. Services provided by these detachments include control tower and TACAN instrument approaches and departures.

(c) MMT.

•The MMT can provide nonradar ATC services up to 40 nautical miles (NM) from a TLZ using a portable NAVAIDS and nonradar procedures. The MMT's relatively small logistic footprint requires fewer transportation assets than the larger MATCD option and is conducive to rapid site establishment and retrogrades. The MMT has a 72-hour capability without resupply or augmentation. It is capable of supporting a variety of ATC missions as an independent unit or as a part of a larger force in joint/multinational operations. The MMT is specifically designed for insertion into remote locations to support MAGTF air operations. Common methods of insertion include—

••Tactical Vehicle. Tactical vehicle insertion is the primary method of deploying a MMT to its air point. To facilitate movement of personnel and equipment to the air point, each MMT is equipped with a high mobility multipurpose wheeled vehicle (HMMWV). Normally, all MMT personnel and equipment will fit within the HMMWV.

••Air Insert. Air insert operations deliver the MMT to their assigned air point by fixed- or rotary-wing aircraft. During these operations, the MMT is typically inserted with the first air element into the objective area. The early establishment of ATC service at the air point ensures that all succeeding aviation elements have ATC and navigational guidance available, thus enhancing the safe and expeditious flow of air traffic into and out of the air point and surrounding airspace.

•As a stand-alone unit distinctive from the MATCD, the MMT is typically task organized to provide ATC services for airfield seizures, noncombatant evacuation operations (NEO), humanitarian/civil assistance operations, and other MEU operations. The MMT is specifically trained and task organized to—

••Recommend/assist in TLZ and HLZ site selection.

••Conduct TLZ/HLZ operations.

••Mark TLZ/HLZ.

••Provide ATC service at designated TLZs/HLZs.

••Coordinate with civil and military control agencies.

•MAGTF Support. The MMT supports the MAGTF by performing the following tasks:

••Formulating and issuing ATC clearances, instructions, and advisories to effect safe, orderly, and expeditious movement of air traffic in their assigned airspace.

••Surveying air sites to determine each site's operational suitability for both numbers and types of aircraft.

••Marking TLZs/HLZs as the mission dictates.

••Establishing a control point from which to exercise ATC.

••Establishing a terminal control area (TCA) around each TLZ and controlling all air traffic within this area under VFR and IFR conditions. This task may be extended to include nonradar approach control services.

••Developing terminal instrument procedures from TLZs/HLZs.

••Providing and operating NAVAIDS.

••Providing limited weather observations and information.

••Assisting in the selection of sites for TLZ/HLZ operations.

•Establishing communications for ATC and ATC coordination within the TCA and for MMT connectivity with the MACCS.

(4) Expeditionary Operations.

Coordination of MAGTF air operations during MEF-sized operations requires a considerable amount of ATC support. It will typically be based on the number of FOBs from which Marine aircraft are operating. Normally, 4 full MATCDs will deploy in support of a MEF to provide continuous, all-weather ATC services at up to 4 main air bases. The 4 detachments can also field 4 MMTs to provide limited ATC services at air facilities or air sites as required. Two MATCDs normally support the forward element of a MEF. The 2 detachments can provide continuous, fully capable ATC services at up to 2 main air bases and 2 MMTs for ATC support at 2 air facilities or air sites. A SPMAGTF is normally supported by a task-organized MATCD ranging in capability from an MMT to a full MATCD. The SPMAGTF's mission and tasks are situational dependent. Limited ATC services are typically provided to the MEU by one MMT. The MMT's mission and tasks are dependent on the situation.

The MAGTF commander uses MAGTF aviation to assist efforts in support of the commander, amphibious task force (CATF), the naval expeditionary force (NEF) commander, or the JFC in preparing and defending the battlespace. In its most common employment, the MATCD will operate in support of expeditionary operations ashore. Each MATCD has the capability of supporting one remote air site or point. The detachment has a full range of ATC capabilities to include—air surveillance radar, identification, friend or foe (IFF), automatic carrier landing system (ACLS) radar, communications, NAVAIDS, and control tower.

This equipment provides a MATCD with positive airspace control capabilities out to 60 NM from a main air base using radar control procedures and out to the limits of MACTD designated airspace using nonradar procedures (procedural control).

Elements of the MATCD, notable the MMT and liaison officers, may be among the first MACCS air control capabilities introduced ashore. MMTs used in either a stand-alone role or as a precursor for a buildup for a larger MATCD are initially established to coincide with initiation of FOB air operations. As airfields are secured, additional ATC capabilities may be phased in to the amphibious objective area (AOA)/area of operation (AO) to provide additional, continuous ATC services for Marine, joint, and allied service aircraft operating from AOA/AO airfields. In situations where MAGTF aviation elements are forward based at an allied nation's airfield located in proximity to the AOA/AO, MATCD personnel may be assigned as liaisons to the host nation's ATC administration. With the introduction of ATC radars into the MAGTF's AO, the MATCD will coordinate for the requisite voice and data links necessary to contribute to the force's IADS through the Marine sector antiair warfare coordinator (SAWC), or as may be designated by the joint force air component commander (JFACC).

d. Equipment.

The MATCD equipment consists of the Marine Air Traffic Control and Landing System (MATCALS), NAVAIDS ATC towers, mobile electric power (MEP), and maintenance shelters. The MATCALS shares various characteristics with the Air Force's (AF's) deployable air traffic control and landing system (DATCALS) that is discussed later in this publication. MATCD equipment is deployed by conventional ground, rail, air, and sealift means. Additionally, United States Marine Corps (USMC) CH-53E helicopters can transport all MATCD equipment. All MATCD radars and communications-electronics shelters are considered oversized cargo. A principal concern when deploying the MATCD is ensuring that adequate transportation and materiels handling equipment (MHE) are available to support the carriers loading and off loading, movement to the site, and equipment emplacement.

The MATCALS provides continuous radar approach, arrival/departure, and en route ATC capabilities. MATCALS collects, evaluates, and displays air track data and disseminates information to other air control agencies. MATCALS consists of three subsystems: AN/TPS-73, air traffic control subsystem, AN/TPN-22; all-weather landing subsystem (ALS); and the AN/TSQ-131, control and communications subsystem (CCS). A description of these systems and a variety of other MATCD systems and equipment are contained in Appendix E.

e. Acquisition Programs. Planned improvements to Marine ATC equipment include the remote landing site tower (RLST) and the common aviation command and control system (CAC2S) described below:

(1) RSLT. The RLST is intended as a replacement for the AN/TRC-195 control central. The RLST will provide the means for rapid emplacement, establishment, and withdrawal of communication and other related capabilities required for VFR ATC services at remote landing sites. The RLST will consist of an extendible roof S-250 shelter containing the equipment required for ATC services at remote sites. The system will include a high-mobility trailer to carry antennas, generators, and communications equipment. The RLST will be capable of operating in an HMMWV-mounted configuration or in a stand-alone configuration. The RLST system will include 6 radios and has the capability to introduce up to 6 landlines into its communication subsystem.

(2) CAC2S. The CAC2S and its communications suite may replace the AN/TSQ-131 upon the end of its service life. The CAC2S initiative will provide a common equipment suite within the MACCS, thus enhancing interoperability and reducing logistics requirements. CAC2S's standardized hardware suite will be equipped with an MACCS-common complement of servers, workstations,

processors, etc. CAC2S's software will consist of standardized common components with agency specific (TACC, TAOC, DASC, etc.) applications. Each system will be modular in design and configured to meet each agency's mission requirements.

f. Training. Marine Corps air traffic controller training is conducted at Naval Air Technical Training Center (NATTC) Pensacola, Florida, in the Air Traffic Controller "A" Course and 2 Air Traffic Controller "C" Courses. See Figure I-4.

(1) Air Traffic Controller Course. Basic ATC trainees receive instruction in the Air Traffic Controller Course, A1. Officers and enlisted personnel receive 14 weeks of training. The trainees receive the basic skills and knowledge required to perform routine duties in the control and handling of aircraft in a tower and radar environment.

(2) Local Training. Upon successful completion of this course, personnel are assigned to an ATC facility (or a MACS for reservists assigned to the 4th Marine Air Wing [MAW], New Orleans, Louisiana). At their assigned duty station, enlisted personnel receive further training and become qualified for military occupational specialty (MOS) 7252 Air Traffic Controller-Tower or MOS 7253 Air Traffic Controller-Radar and officers become qualified for MOS 7220 ATC Officer. This training combines "OJT" and formal instruction.

(3) Advanced Radar ATC Course. Selected air traffic controllers receive 9 weeks of training in Course C1, Advanced Radar ATC (ARATC). This phase of training provides students with the skill and knowledge to perform at a basic level as radar approach controller at all operating positions at a radar approach facility.

(4) MATCALS Basic Operators Course. This is a 1-week course that provides Marine ATC personnel with familiarization training on the MATCALS following entry level schooling. Marines

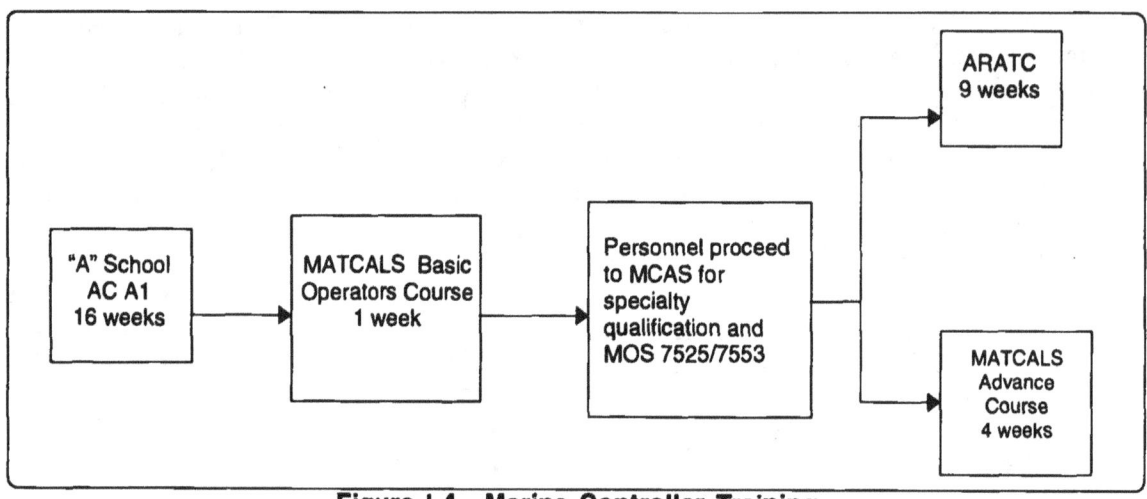

Figure I-4. Marine Controller Training

receive instruction on the operation of MATCALS equipment and are introduced to the mission and structure of Marine aviation.

(5) MATCALS Advanced Operators Course. This is a 4-week course that provides senior Marine ATC personnel with comprehensive training on the employment and operation of MATCALS. Students receive instruction on the operation, capabilities, and limitations of the MATCALS. Students are also instructed on developing/designing US Standard TERPS.

4. Navy

a. Doctrine.

(1) Amphibious Control. There are basically two levels of operations for the tactical air control group (TACGRU), tactical air control squadron (TACRON), or tactical air control detachments. They are identified as MEU or MEF level operations. MEUs comprise the landing force for an amphibious ready group. TACGRU/TACRON support for MEU level operations will normally consist of a detachment. MEFs, as part of an amphibious task force, are much larger and often have special support requirements and TACGRU/TACRON support for these levels of operations will be necessary to successfully complete the mission.

(a) TACRON. Typically, a TACRON deploys as one of numerous embarked elements onboard an amphibious carrier. The detachment officer-in-charge (OIC) is normally assigned as the amphibious commander's air officer. The amphibious squadron commander is operationally in command of the amphibious ready group (ARG). The ARG also has a MEU assigned, which consists of approximately 2000 marines in ground, air, and support elements. An ARG is capable of landing and supporting combat troops from both the air and sea. The ARG may consist of a variety of ships to include—

•General purpose amphibious assault ship (LHA).

•General purpose amphibious assault ship (with transport dock)—(LHD).

•Amphibious assault ship, landing platform helicopter (LPH).

•Landing ship dock (LSD).

•Amphibious transport dock (LPD).

(b) Tactical Air Control Center (TACC). When an amphibious operation has been identified and an AOA or AOR has been delineated (including all of its control points), the TACRON becomes responsible for the control/monitoring/coordination of all fixed-wing assets entering, exiting, or operating within the assigned area. Typically this function is performed in the

TACC aboard LHA/LHD/LPH class ships. Control of helicopters is generally retained by the ship's air operations control center (AOCC)/helicopter direction center (HDC). All aircraft will check in with the tactical air traffic controller (TATC) before entering assigned airspace in order to receive control instructions, traffic deconfliction, mission information/briefing, and transfer to subsequent control agencies. Transition control may be a function of another individual (the tactical air director [TAD]) within the TACC or it may be an outside agency. Following mission completion, aircraft will check out of the area via the TATC in order to ensure that required information is passed to aircrews.

(2) Aircraft Carrier Control. Airspace around a carrier battle group (CVBG) is monitored, controlled, and defended by the air warfare commander (AWC). The AWC is usually the commanding officer of an AEGIS Cruiser or Destroyer. The AWC releases operational taskings (OPTASKs) and daily intention messages that describe the air posture, airspace restrictions, and general air procedures to be followed by CVBG air assets. The AWC usually has in place a positive identification and radar advisory zone (PIRAZ). The AWC and PIRAZ control units are usually collocated. A PIRAZ allows the AWC to identify all aircraft operating in the defended area as well as maintain track integrity. The PIRAZ circuit is UHF, usually callsign "RED-CROWN." "RED-CROWN" should be contacted when entering or exiting airspace around a CVBG.

(a) Carrier Air Traffic Control Center (CATCC).

Carrier ATC is the mission of the CATCC. Navy air traffic controllers man the CATCC. CATCC positions include approach, departure, marshal, and final control. All ATC control frequencies and various administrative circuits for special aircrew information/instructions are UHF. During VMC conditions, the tower controls airspace within 5 miles of the carrier. Aircraft requesting landing, transit, or fly-by must contact the tower before entering this airspace. Additionally, a 50-mile radius around the carrier is considered the control area and is under the control of CATCC and the combat direction center (CDC).

Frequencies for CATCC, *RED-CROWN*, *STRIKE*, and the tower can be found in the standing OPTASK communications, daily-intentions messages, or carrier communication kneeboard cards. Special instructions (SPINS) often list some of these frequencies when a CVBG is operating in support of a joint operation.

(b) Air Resource Element Coordinator (AREC). In addition to CATCC, AREC maintains an administrative UHF circuit for passing aircraft status, amending recovery times, coordinating nonorganic assets (for example, KC-135, etc.). This circuit is called STRIKE. This is controlled by the tactical actions officer (TAO).

b. Forces. Forces available for naval ATC operations are derived from two TACGRUs as depicted in Appendix A. TACGRUs or TACRONs will deploy aboard amphibious flag or amphibious command ships for operations in direct support of amphibious task force operations when directed. They are responsible for providing centralized command, control, and planning coordination of all air support and airspace required for amphibious operations for numbered fleet commanders. When the TACGRU/TACRON deploys, it will be composed of elements of each TACRON or the entire group.

(1) TACRON. Typically a TACRON has approximately 15-20 officers and 60-70 enlisted personnel assigned. Officer manning is comprised of naval aviators and naval flight officers of nearly every warfare specialty and Marine aviators. Enlisted

manning consists primarily of air traffic controllers and operations specialists (OS), but squadrons also have personnel assigned to provide operational and administrative support. Some of the important positions in the TACRON and its detachments are described in Appendix F.

(a) Organization. Ashore, the TACRON is typically organized like any other command with administrative operations, training, and other supporting departments. Detachment composition while deployed generally is OIC (0-5) and 4-5 other officers and 18-22 enlisted personnel. Manning will vary somewhat, depending on the ship embarked.

(b) Deployment. The commanding officer of a TACRON will deploy in support of amphibious group commanders as the TAO. The TACRON will man and operate a TACC to provide centralized planning, control, coordination, and integration of all air operations in support of amphibious operations, training, and transits. Each squadron is currently capable of providing two detachments a year with a projected cycle of 6 months deployed and 12 months in port as directed by the Chief of Naval Operations (CNO). Detachments are required continuously.

(2) TACC. The TACRON detachments, as operational units of a TACRON, will deploy in support of amphibious squadron commanders. The detachment OIC shall serve as the TAO. The detachment will staff and operate the TACC to provide centralized planning control coordination and integration of all air operations in support of amphibious operations, training, and transits. A detachment will be tailored to meet the tasking and will reflect the ship type assigned for the deployment. TACC is divided into the following five functional areas (sections):

(a) Helicopter Coordination Section (HCS). The HCS is responsible for the coordination of all helicopter operations conducted by HDCs and other subordinate control agencies within the amphibious ready group and the operational control of specific helicopter missions when required.

(b) Air Traffic Control Section (ATCS). This section is responsible for controlling all air traffic entering, operating within, or traversing the assigned operating area and for coordination of search and rescue (SAR) operations.

(c) Air Support Control Section (ASCS). ASCS is responsible for controlling all fixed- and rotary-wing aircraft assigned to close and deep air support missions.

(d) Air Warfare Section (AWS). AWS is responsible for coordinating and evaluating all air warning reports and controlling all air warfare assets including fighter aircraft, antiaircraft missiles and guns, and electronic attack assigned. Supervises qualified TACRON, flagship, and staff personnel that are integrated into the AWS.

(e) Plans and Support Section (PSS). PSS is responsible for all communications support, conducts current and future planning, and assembles and distributes current air operations data and reports.

c. Capabilities. The TACRONs operate in and as part of a joint or unified force. They are capable of operating as an element of the JFACC, providing air control and planning in a unified or multinational theater of operations. Helicopters are employed in the moving of troops and materiel ashore while fixed-wing aircraft provide close air support (CAS) for friendly ground forces and ensure air superiority by employing combat air patrols (CAP). They are capable of performing all assigned primary missions simultaneously while maintaining continuous readiness conditions I, IA, III (wartime/deployment/cruising readiness) or IV (peacetime steaming) at sea, and V (in port).

Appendix G contains detailed information on their primary missions and capabilities. In addition, the TACRONs maintain the capability to temporarily staff and operate an existing ATC facility ashore or augment a remote facility ashore with personnel to control air traffic in support of emergency or disaster relief operations.

d. Equipment. With the exception of PRC-113s, TACRONs do not *own* any ATC equipment. Amphibious ATC equipment is *installed* on LHA-1 (*Tarawa*-San Diego), LHA-2 (*Saipan*-Norfolk), LHA-3 (*Belleau Wood*-Japan), LHA-4 (*Nassau*-Norfolk), LHA-5 (*Peleliu*-San Diego), LHD-1 (*Wasp*-Norfolk), LHD-2 (*Essex*-San Diego), LHD-3 (*Kearsarge*-Norfolk), LHD-4 (*Boxer*-San Diego), LHD-5 (*Bataan*-Norfolk), and LHD-6 (*Bon Homme Richard*-San Diego). Appendix E provides additional details on Navy ATC equipment.

e. Acquisition Programs. Current displays are undergoing updating on several ships. Some updating has been completed.

f. Training.

(1) General. Consistent with the Navy's mission, training is oriented toward all aspects of ATC to provide a competent sea and shore based training program. This section outlines all aspects of Navy ATC training to allow comparison/familiarity by other personnel and other users of this publication.

(2) Population. Navy/Marine ATC personnel are located around the globe at Naval/Marine Corps Air Stations, CATCC aboard every aircraft carrier (CV/CVN), AOCC aboard every large deck amphibious ship (LHA/LHD/LPH) and TACRONs. In addition, there are unique locations such as fleet area control and surveillance facility (FACSFAC) that are responsible for US-based over-water control of fleet air assets. In general, where Navy ATC personnel are required to fill land-based positions as directed by the JFC, the only

land-based Navy ATC combat control would be provided by a shore-based TACRON detachment. All TACRON organizations and capabilities are outlined in Appendices D and E. Familiarity with the information contained in these appendices is needed if a non-United States Navy (USN) ATC organization is expected to assume control of established TACRON ATC operations.

(3) Courses. All phases of Navy air traffic controller training are conducted at NATTC, Pensacola, Florida. Initial ATC training consists of 14 weeks of basic AC "A1" school. This is the foundation of the controller training process. Upon graduation, Navy controllers possess the basic skills and core knowledge of FAA ATC procedures in both tower and radar facilities.

(a) Advanced Courses. Additionally, there are 3 ATC advanced courses, CATCC Operations (CV/CVN personnel), AOCC Operations (TACRON and LHA/LHD/LPH/MCS personnel), and ARATC (approach control personnel). Advanced courses are all approximately 6 weeks in length. In most instances, newly designated Navy air traffic controllers attend advanced ATC courses immediately after AC "A1" school, while senior controllers attend when en route to their next duty assignment. CATCC operations and AOCC operations courses both offer a 2-week team training course that is used to provide refresher training necessary to retain overall team performance and individual skill proficiency in performing ATC operations at sea. The appropriate fleet type commander schedules this course throughout the year. Refer to Appendix C for a matrix that outlines specific training objectives, schools, qualifications, etc.

(b) Proficiency Courses. JATC planners must understand there are 2 types of proficiency training necessary to bring any ATC personnel up to maximum efficiency: *qualification* training and *proficiency* training. *Qualification* training refers to obtaining the initial qualification training to achieve an initial level of proficiency. *Proficiency* training refers to training on specific ATC equipment to achieve proficiency on that particular equipment. Proficiency training can also be related to learning specific local area procedures and including standard operating procedures (SOP), flight advisories, etc. See Appendix C for more details.

5. Air Force

a. Doctrine. The USAF provides ATC services to support theater tactical combat operations and combat airspace management similar to what the Service's fixed base facilities provide in the continental United States (CONUS) and overseas. The USAF ATC is involved in a multitude of missions from combat to MOOTW. Reserve components play a key role in ATC operations and in some cases could be tasked instead of active duty forces. However, currently there is no specific AF doctrine directing the execution of ATC and the transition from initial to transition and subsequently sustained operations. Recent operations in central Europe and the Middle East have essentially demonstrated all 3 phases but there was little evident difference between them. The equipment initially deployed was, in most cases, used during all phases of the operations, and personnel numbers and qualifications changed little from phase to phase. There was also no handoff from one type or classification of assets to another.

b. Forces. Special tactics (ST) forces provide the initial ATC capability and execute missions for both SOF and conventional forces/operations. ST forces are ground combat forces assigned to Air Force Special Operations Command (AFSOC), Hurlburt Field, Florida. Special tactics forces consist of combat control, pararescue, and combat weather personnel who are organized, trained, and equipped to establish and control the air-ground interface and provide airmanship skills in the objective area. Combat controllers provide the ATC capability. Combat controllers are parachute and combat diver qualified personnel trained and equipped to quickly establish and control terminal air objectives (DZs or LZs) in austere or hostile environments. They perform reconnaissance, surveillance, and survey and assessment of potential terminal airheads (airfields or assault zones). They conduct ATC, terminal attack control, and initial C2 communications during assault operations. They can also perform limited weather observations and obstacle or ordinance removal with demolitions. Specific ST units are listed in Appendix H. ST forces provide a unique capability and deploy with air and joint ground forces in the execution of direct action (DA), counterterrorism (CT), foreign internal defense (FID), humanitarian assistance (HA), special reconnaissance (SR), personnel recovery (PR), and austere airfield operations missions. To permit the positive C2 of forward operations, ST forces are attached as staff and tactical liaisons to supported ground force units at the company, battalion, and regimental level and at the joint/multinational task force level.

c. Capabilities.

(1) Special Tactics Teams (STT).

STTs of the special tactics squadrons (STSs) are rapidly deployable, highly mobile forces capable of providing VMC/limited IMC ATC and limited airfield operations for austere, expeditionary airfields. Teams are task organized with the most common task organizations unit type code (UTC) packaged. They are worldwide deployable to a main base or forward operating location within 12 hours of notification. Teams will require host support at the deployed location. The team leader tailors the exact team composition and equipment to meet specific mission requirements. However, the force is also structured to use smaller mission specific UTCs. These UTCs are capable of being tactically inserted directly into the objective area in order to provide ATC service using a variety of methods: static line or military free-fall parachute; scuba, small boat, or amphibious means; overland, using mounted or dismounted techniques; airland, via fixed- or rotary-wing aircraft; airmobile procedures, including rope, ladder, or stabo.

ST forces can be employed as stand-alone units or combined with other SOF into a joint team and perform the following JATC related mission tasks:

(a) Assault Zone (AZ) Assessment. Select, evaluate, survey, and establish AZs. The STT can—

•Clear, mark, and operate the AZ for fixed- and rotary-wing aircraft.

•Establish en route and terminal precision and nonprecision NAVAIDS and beacons.

•Conduct reconnaissance and surveillance airfield and AZ objectives.

•Support selected regional survey team (RST) missions.

•Remove obstacles to flight for transition operations.

(b) Austere Airfield Control. Provide terminal guidance and ATC to the AZ under VFR and limited IFR (nonradar) conditions. The team can—

•Establish ground-to-air communications.

•Coordinate AZ activities with the ground force commander.

•Perform weather observations.

•Provide positive control of personnel and equipment within the airhead area, to include control of FARP operations.

(2) Combat Communications Support. Limited numbers of active duty air traffic controllers are assigned to DATCALS at two CONUS-based Air Combat Command (ACC) combat communications groups (CCGs). ATC augmentees must be sourced from major command (MAJCOM) UTC-tasked fixed base assets to operate in a deployed environment (see Appendix A). The assets assigned to CCG units include both maintenance personnel and CCG equipment. Conversely, in Air National Guard (ANG) ATC units, air traffic controllers, and maintainers are in packages separate from their associated DATCALS.

(3) Fixed Base ATC Support. The preponderance of controllers are located at CONUS fixed base locations and assigned to facility-specific UTCs designed to support a wide range of ATC taskings. Fixed base controllers are identified and trained to support control tower, radar approach control (RAPCON), as well as ATC liaison requirements. Limited VFR control tower services may be provided using AN/MRC-144 assets assigned to select ACC wing initial communications package (WIC-P) using available wing ATC assets.

(4) General Purpose Air Traffic Controllers. The limited number of air traffic controllers assigned to CCGs are generally equipped but do not usually provide initial bare base ATC services. Select ACC WIC-Ps also contain MRC-144 assets and could provide VFR-tower services using controller assets from the wing they are supporting.

(a) DATCALS. DATCALS provide ATC service and positive control capabilities in the combat zone to both the air and land component commanders. DATCALS (ANG and active duty) deployment characteristics are such that they deploy with organic maintenance and logistic support, which contributes to their deployability, flexibility, and responsiveness. ANG controllers normally deploy with their equipment. Most of the controllers operating active duty systems are provided from CONUS-based fixed ATC facilities. Both personnel and equipment require significant airlift or surface transportation for deployment.

(b) DATCALS Integration. The MAJCOMs/numbered Air Forces (NAFs) should promote "joint" exercises and ensure integration of the DATCALS into training exercises whenever feasible. Exercises should use realistic planning, deployment, and maintenance training for DATCALS UTCs. Field exercises whereby deployable equipment usage and skills are taught are important in the training process to practice how we will fight. UTCs tasked to support DATCALS and combat airspace/liaison positions must be indoctrinated through exercises before "real-world" deployments if they will be responsible for establishing/managing these systems while deployed.

d. Equipment.

(1) Commonly Used Equipment. Appendix E contains a list and description of the most commonly used AF ATC equipment which includes—

(a) The AN/TPN-19 Landing Control Central (radar set) can be configured as a complete RAPCON or GCA facility.

(b) The AN/TRN-26 or AN/TRN-41 TACAN is designed to provide radio navigation information (bearing, identification, and distance) at remote landing strips and forward operating areas.

(c) The AN/TSW-7 Tower Central is a mobile control tower used to provide ATC capabilities where no control tower exists (bare base operations) or where the fixed control tower is not operational. This will be replaced by the AN/MSN-7 Tower Restoral Vehicle.

(d) The AN/MRC-144 Mobile HF/VHF/UHF communications facility (AN/GRC-206) mounted in an M-988 HMMWV provides limited VFR control tower operations when used in an ATC capacity.

(2) DATCALS Equipment. ANG sustainment DATCALS packages consist of the following:

(a) The AN/MPN-14K Landing Control Central (radar set) can be configured as a complete RAPCON or GCA facility. Though it is mobile, it is not designed to be moved frequently.

(b) AN/TRN-26 (see above).

(c) The AN/TSW-7 (see above) is currently being replaced by the AN/MSN-7 Tower Restoral Vehicle (TRV).

(3) Special Tactics Equipment.

The equipment assigned to ST forces is either packable or highly mobile on all terrain vehicles (ATV) or the MRC-144 communications vehicles. The equipment can be deployed to mark and control runways and includes portable airfield lighting, UHF/VHF/HF/SATCOM/FM communications, TACAN, portable beacons and NAVAIDS, and a mobile microwave landing system (MMLS).

The core UTC package can provide ATC services for up to 14 days and includes 18 personnel, MRC-144's, ATVs, NAVAIDS, portable radios, survey equipment, and portable airfield lighting. Resupply of consumable items is required if operations are extended past 14 days. This UTC can be deployed on one C-141. Additional information on ST equipment and capabilities can be found in Appendix H.

(4) Flight Inspection. The DOD flight inspection capability for contingency or combat operations was included in the FAA flight inspection program in the 1998 USAF/FAA Memorandum of Agreement (MOA). This agreement transferred 6 aircraft and aircrews from the USAF to the FAA. The FAA uses the assigned USAF and USAFR personnel and aircraft to flight

inspect navigational aids outside the scope of FAA planned activities (that is, combat or contingency operations). This includes flight inspections of TACANs, VORTACs, VORs, nondirectional beacons (NDBs), MLS, instrument landing system (ILS), and ATC radar, approach airfield lighting and other navigational aids. These flight inspections ensure NAVAIDS meet signal quality and accuracy parameters and instrument approach procedures and obstacle clearance criteria are met. (See Chapter II, 6b(3)(b).

e. Acquisition Programs. The current deployable ATC systems are composed of numerous electronic components, several produced in the 1950s. Key elements of the AF ATC inventory are justified to support current war plans and operate a fully integrated ATC system, including mobile control towers, radar approach controls, navigational aids, communications equipment, and airfield lighting. These systems are becoming technologically obsolete and expensive to maintain as they near the end of their projected service life. Programmed modifications may extend that service life but do not adequately address modernization to meet current/future ATC needs. For example, planned modifications for the TPN-19 will only maintain its current operational capability and operability. It does not address the need to be compatible with FAA and International Civil Aviation Organization (ICAO) long-term efforts.

(1) Current.

The USAF is currently in the testing stage for procurement of Tower Restoral Vehicles (AN/MSN-7). The AN/MSN-7 is designed to replace active duty and ANG AN/TSW-7 assets. Thirty-seven MMLSs have been procured and 33 are now being fielded. The USAF is coordinating an operational requirements document (ORD) to define a replacement for existing mobile radar systems.

The FAA, along with the ICAO, is currently implementing plans that will revolutionize the world's communications, navigation, and surveillance systems. The entire worldwide air traffic system will evolve from a ground-based to space-based system (for example, ground-based NAVAIDS like the TACAN will be replaced with the GPS, and ground-based control centers will transmit ATC instructions to and receive aircraft position information from the space-based system) driving changes in both avionics and ground equipment requirements. The AF sees the *number one priority* in ATC as updating or replacing outdated and hard to maintain systems in order to continue to provide the same service as the FAA and host nations. This need is being addressed in parallel with the FAA and ICAO upgrades started in 1997 and continuing through 2010. Sustainment of current DATCALS while transitioning to the new architecture will allow for a smooth transfer of function without degrading existing ATC and navigation services until all US military aircraft have completed appropriate avionics upgrades.

Mobile components should be configured and sized for deployment so as to minimize airlift requirements while still providing the functionality of current systems.

(2) Future. To provide the capability for fixed base and mobile operations into the next century, the system must accept multiple sensor input (ground-based, airborne, and space-based) and be fully interoperable with existing and forecasted DOD command, control, communications, and computer (C4) systems. Additionally, it must be capable of interfacing with airfield defense (data and voice) and National Airspace Systems (NAS) facilities (analog and digital data). Because of the operations in foreign countries, the new fixed and mobile system must be fully interoperable with FAA, ICAO, and North Atlantic Treaty Organization (NATO) current and developing ATC systems.

f. Training.

(1) General Training. USAF ATC training is conducted at Keesler Technical Training Center, Biloxi, Mississippi. The foundation of the controller training process is the ATC technical training center. Upon graduation, apprentice controllers possess basic skills and core knowledge of FAA ATC procedures. These fundamentals and principals are expanded upon in unit training programs and with meeting local unit facility and qualification training requirements. Training requirements for all AF controllers are defined in AFI 13-203, Chapter 6. The scope of unit training programs and the qualifications ATC personnel must possess are determined by the type(s) of ATC facilities, number of operating positions, and volume and type of local air operations at the unit of assignment. FAA-approved USAF examiners assigned to and fully qualified at the trainee's facility certify members. Training parameters are also tailored to the facility based on average times for previous trainees (adjusted annually), prior or non-prior ratings, and positions being trained. *Position Certification Guides* (PCGs) present the trainee with a phased approach that builds on simple tasks and progress to complex. *Task Certification Guides (TCGs)* specify advanced training requirements such as local watch supervisor, TERPS, airspace management (at larger bases), etc. PCGs and TCGs contain core tasks from the USAF Job Qualification Standard as well as local procedures. In building PCGs or TCGs, facility managers use the principles contained in AFI 36-2234, *Instructional Systems Development*. Each facility manager determines the maximum time spent in each block to ensure quality, yet timely training progress, which can result in vastly different upgrade times between facilities. Upon initial assignment, all USAF apprentice air traffic controllers incur mandatory orientation training during the first 90 days of assignment as required by the 1993 Year of Training initiatives. Specific AF controller qualifications such as combat airspace management, TERPS, supervisory positions, etc., are identified by a special experience identifier (SEI). A SEI is a 3-digit numerical code used to identify controller qualifications or controllers with special skills. SEIs are awarded to AF controllers who meet the designated facility qualification requirements. Additional SEIs are awarded upon completion of the Joint Air Operations Staff Course, Military Airspace Management Course, or TERPS Course, and applicable job qualification standards. SEIs are critical to the AF ATC planning process as they can identify controllers who meet the specific ATC qualification requirements at a deployed location. When SEIs are not used, poor utilization of controllers can result in greatly extended training time and degraded service to air operations at the deployed location. See Table I-1.

(2) Unit Training. Personnel and equipment training is also integrated into unit training plans. Individual bases are responsible for providing/funding combat readiness training and equipment. This training should include standard mobility requirements such as government motor vehicle training, chemical warfare training, weapons training, and proper mobilization procedures to include personnel processing, airlift load preparation, and palletizing. Training requirements for personnel subject to or identified for deployment are defined in AFI 10-403. The AF's objective is to ensure an institutionalized and standardized AF training program, which spans across all MAJCOMs. ACC, having the largest number of controllers of any command, has its own combat skills course dedicated to producing more deployment-oriented controllers. The concept is to use a three phased approach: (1) Predeployment training-training required to be assigned to UTC, (2) in-residence combat skills course to teach survival skills, and equipment familiarization under field conditions, and (3) exercises-to practice and apply what has been learned. Initial training is usually conducted in an austere environment such

as a forward base during war (DESERT SHIELD/STORM); a disaster area (Homestead Air Force Base, Florida, after Hurricane Andrew); or any other MOOTW (drug interdiction fields, foreign humanitarian operations, etc.). This training usually consists of a quick orientation of the airdrome and airspace and is tailored to the controller's prior experience. As the airfield operations mature and procedures become more standardized, the facility managers are charged with developing a local training plan for controllers rotating in theater to support sustained operations.

Table I-1. USAF ATC SEIs

OFFICER	
Position	SEI
Airfield Management	OCH
Combat Airspace Management	OCK
Airspace Management	OUL
ENLISTED	
Position	SEI
Tower Controller	056
Tower Watch Supervisor	055
GCA Controller	053
GCA Supervisor	054
Radar Approach Controller	364
Radar Approach Control Watch Supervisor	362
Air Route Traffic Control Center	363
Airspace Management	350
Combat Airspace Management	900
Precision Approach Radar (PAR)	365
TERPS	361

Chapter II

OPERATIONS AND PROCEDURES

1. Background

This chapter describes how individual Services' ATC capabilities are employed in the joint environment. Unlike flight operations, which normally share an airfield, the ATC support is normally provided by one Service. The individual Services have not previously pursued joint air traffic control (JATC) doctrine and efficiencies nor the enhanced capabilities of combining multiservice ATC functions. This chapter outlines the established joint air operations environment and then discusses individual Service ATC procedures. With this information, the joint planner can better understand the guidance in Chapter III.

2. General Duties, Responsibilities, Communications, and C2 Relationships

a. Duties and Responsibilities. ATC supports worldwide military or other assigned operations at theater command/ commander in chief (CINC) directed locations. Planning for JATC operations begins during mobilization/predeployment to enable the JFC to determine JATC requirements and to allow for sourcing of needed JATC assets. From the outset of the operations, task-organized, tailored force packages normally support the mission by providing JATC services to all military and friendly aircraft in a deployed environment. Facilities, capabilities, and procedures mature as forces deploy and the TAGS is implemented. During and after decisive operations, JATC support and facilities must be sustained based on the factors of METT-T. During all phases of the operation, ATC liaison personnel establish ATC coordination for communications, radar, and C2 with adjacent ATC units and ACAs. Each Service is capable of providing expert airspace management personnel to an ACA. The following guidance outlines duties and responsibilities during a joint operation. See Figure II-1 for a diagram of command relationships.

(1) CINC. Five combatant commanders have geographic areas of responsibility. These combatant commanders are each assigned an AOR by the *Unified Command Plan* and are responsible for all operations within their designated areas: United States European Command (USEUCOM), United States Southern Command (USSOUTHCOM), United States Atlantic Command (USACOM), United States Pacific Command (USPACOM), and United States Central Command (USCENTCOM). The CINCs of the remaining combatant commands have worldwide functional responsibilities not bounded by geography: United States Special Operations Command (USSOCOM), United States Transportation Command (USTRANSCOM), United States Space Command (USSPACECOM), and United States Strategic Command (USSTRATCOM). Theater CINCs exercise combatant command over assigned and attached units. Each unified command has a Service component representing the needs, interests, and Service-unique expertise to the CINC. The CINC (through the staff and components) determines initial ATC requirements at specific deployment locations based upon the operational requirements.

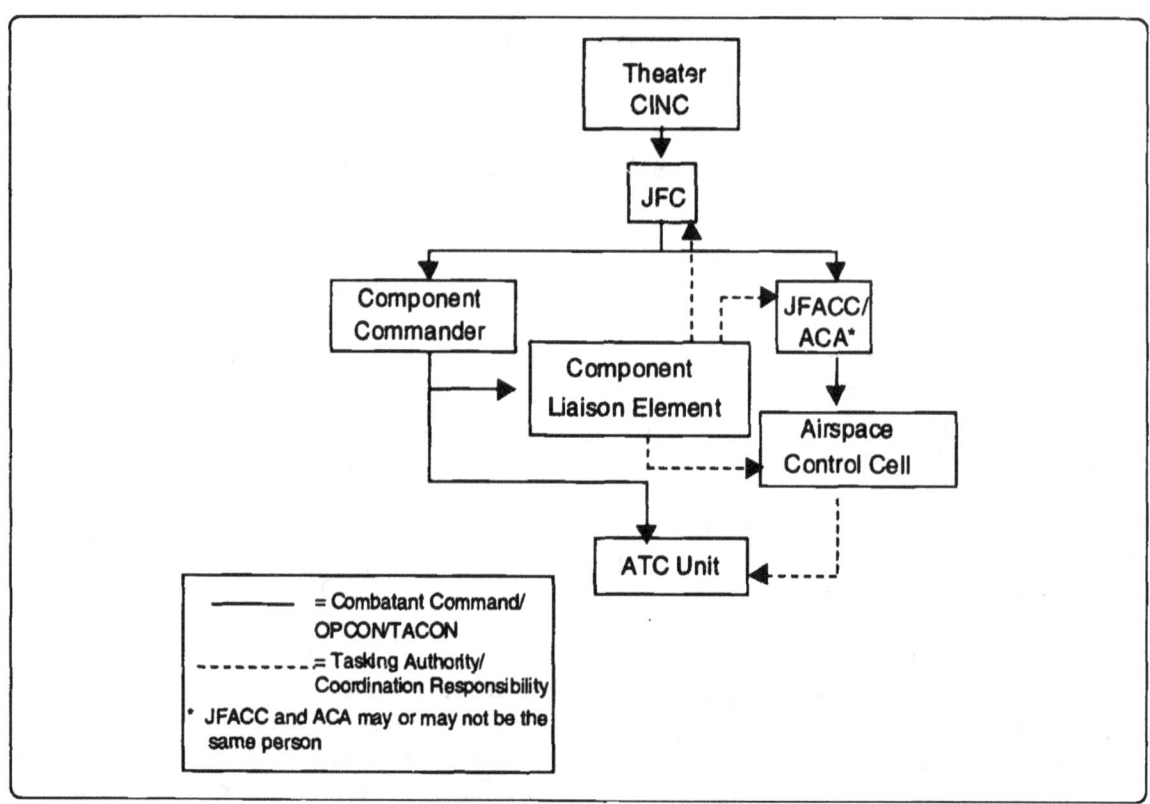

Figure II-1. Command Relationships

(2) JFC. JFC is a general term applied to a combatant commander, subunified commander, or JTF commander authorized to exercise combatant command (command authority) or operational control over a joint force (Joint Publication 1-02). In addition, the JFC exercises operational control (OPCON) over assigned forces, and normally over attached forces, to include ATC forces. The JFC directs employment of ATC assets and handoff of responsibility from one unit to another (single service, joint, coalition, or host nation) through the ACP, published by the ACA. Additionally, the JFC establishes requirements for liaisons in interservice, coalition, and host nation facilities.

(3) Joint Force Air Component Commander (JFACC). The JFACC derives authority from the JFC who has the authority to exercise operational control, assign missions, direct coordination among subordinate commanders, redirect and organize forces to ensure unity of effort in the accomplishment of the overall mission.

The JFACC's responsibilities will be assigned by the JFC (normally those include, but not limited to, planning, coordination, allocation, and tasking based on the JFC's apportionment decision). Using the JFC's guidance and authority and in coordination with other Service component commanders and other assigned or supporting commanders, the JFACC will recommend to the JFC apportionment of air sorties to various missions or geographic areas (Joint Publication 1-02).

(4) ACA. ACA is the commander designated to assume overall responsibility for the operation of ACS in the airspace control area (Joint Publication 1-02). Broad responsibilities include coordinating and integrating the use of the airspace control area, establishing an ACS, and developing the ACP and implementing it through the ACO, which must be complied with by all components. ACA activities are conducted with JFC guidance and with J-3 authority. All missions are subject to the ACO of the ACA; however,

centralized direction by the ACA does not imply OPCON or tactical control (TACON) over any air assets. The ACA promulgates JFC requirements, plans, and tasks for ATC units through the ACP and ACO (see discussion on ACP and ACO, below).

(5) Airspace Control Center. The airspace control center is the ACA's primary airspace control facility, including assigned service component, host nation, and/or allied personnel and equipment (Joint Publication 1-02).

(6) ACS. ACS is an arrangement of those organizations, personnel, policies, and facilities required to perform airspace control functions (Joint Publication 1-02).

(7) Functional Component Command. Functional component command is a command normally, but not necessarily, composed of forces of two or more military departments which may be established across the range of military operations to perform particular operational missions that may be of short duration or may extend over a period of time (Joint Publication 1-02).

(8) Service Component Command. Service component command is a command consisting of the service component commander and all those service forces, such as individuals, units, detachments, organizations, and installations under the command, including the support force that have been assigned to a combatant command or further assigned to a subordinate unified command or joint task force (Joint Publication 1-02). This command retains TACON of component forces and advises JFC on employment of component forces and direction and control of those forces. Service component command functions include—

(a) Coordinating and deconflicting the employment of assigned and attached forces with other subordinate commands as required by the operational situation.

(b) Providing ATC in areas designated by the ACA in accordance with directives and/or procedures in the ACP.

(c) Developing detailed ATC instructions, plans, and procedures in accordance with guidance in the ACP.

(d) Providing necessary facilities and personnel for ATC in assigned areas of operations and identifying these facilities and personnel to the ACA for inclusion in the ACP.

(e) Providing ATC liaisons to the other components to ensure component capabilities, limitations, needs, and desires are considered in planning and execution at all levels of C2.

(9) Component Liaison Elements. The component liaison elements to the JFACC (for example, the special operations liaison element [SOLE], the BCD, naval and amphibious liaison element [NALE], and the Marine liaison officer [MARLO]), may also provide representation to the ACA if the JFACC has been designated the ACA by the JFC or is collocated in the joint air operations center (JAOC). Otherwise, additional liaison elements may be required. ATC representatives in these liaison elements will work with the ACA and airspace management team in the JAOC to ensure the ATC portion of the ACP and ACO has taken capabilities, limitations, needs, and requirements of the components into consideration. All components are not required to send a liaison to the CRC.

(10) ATC Unit. This unit provides ATC service to aircraft operating within airspace defined in the ACP. The unit develops local operating procedures in accordance with ICAO, FAA, host nation, Service specific, and joint directives, as well as the ACP, ATO, ACO and other applicable ACA/JFC instructions. The unit is also responsible for coordinating and establishing communication links with

adjacent air defense units and fire support elements to ensure identification criteria are implemented IAW standing directives and are useable and understandable. The ATC unit also establishes procedures for interoperability with adjacent collateral, subordinate, and superior component, joint, coalition, and host nation ATC facilities.

b. Documents. The following JFC produced documents contain guidance supplemental to ICAO, FAA, host nation, and service specific, and joint directives:

(1) ACP. ACP is the document approved by the JFC that provides specific planning guidance and procedures for the ACS for the joint force area of responsibility/joint operations area (Joint Publication 1-02). The ACP is developed by the ACA and approved by the JFC to establish procedures for the ACS in the joint force AOR/JOA. The ACP must consider procedures and interfaces with the international or regional air traffic systems necessary to effectively support air logistics, augmenting forces, and JFC objectives. One broad area of concern for developing the ACP is familiarity with capabilities and procedures of military and civil ATC systems. The ACP establishes initial ATC system structure, outlines procedures for transition from peacetime to wartime ATC operations (if required), and details procedures for handing ATC responsibility off from one ATC unit to another (if required). The ACP should provide procedures to fully integrate the resources of the military ATC facility responsible for terminal-area airspace control. ATC facilities should be interfaced and linked with ACS communications to form a system that ensures safe efficient flow of air traffic supporting the combat effort while permitting maximum combat flexibility.

(2) ACO. ACO is an order implementing the ACP that provides the details of the approved requests for airspace control measures. It is published either as part of the ATO or as a separate document (Joint Publication 1-02).

(3) SPINS. SPINS provide details of the approved requests for special airspace control measures. It is published either as part of the ATO or as a separate document.

3. Army ATC Duties, Responsibilities, and C2 Relationships

Army ATC provides service and coordination from its mobilization bases in the CONUS and its forward presence units outside of the continental United States (OCONUS). Most contingency operations require strategic air/sealift to effect force projection. As a result, most Army ATS planning is focused on the initial phase of operations in an AOR and the redeployment phase out of the AOR. However, the Army's ability to self-deploy to certain locations requires planners to preplan and coordinate the transit of national and international airspace from point of departure through en route locations to arrival in the AOR. This coordination is done through FAA and ICAO organizations. The Department of Army Regional Representatives (DARRs) at FAA National Regional Headquarters assists with this coordination. There are Army ATS representatives located in OCONUS offices at United States Forces, Korea (USFK) and United States Army, Europe (USAREUR) to coordinate Army requirements in these theaters. As early in the crisis action planning cycle as possible the joint planner must contact the United States Army Forces Command (FORSCOM), Deputy Chief of Staff Operations (DCSOPS) Aviation Staff to initiate ATS asset allocation in support of a joint operation. Once ATS units are notified of their involvement in an operation, the organizations described below must be coordinated with to implement planning guidance. The following describes the responsibilities of Army organizations. See Figure II-2 for the Army ATS structure.

a. ATS Group

(1) Provides C2 of all theater Army ATS assets.

(2) Advises the ARFOR commander on airspace/ATC implementation and employment.

(3) Implements the ARFOR commander's guidance.

(4) Provides liaison teams to the JAOC (J-3 Air), the BCD at the JAOC, and the CRC (theater support company).

(a) Liaison team (LNO team) to J-3 of JOC.

• Joint forces interface.

• Host nation interface.

• Host nation ATC system.

• Provides input to the ACP development which includes—ATC assets deployed/employed initially (initial), plans for relief of initial ATC assets (who and when), plans for air traffic maturation/ sustainment (which facilities remain), and plans for redeployment activities (sustainment).

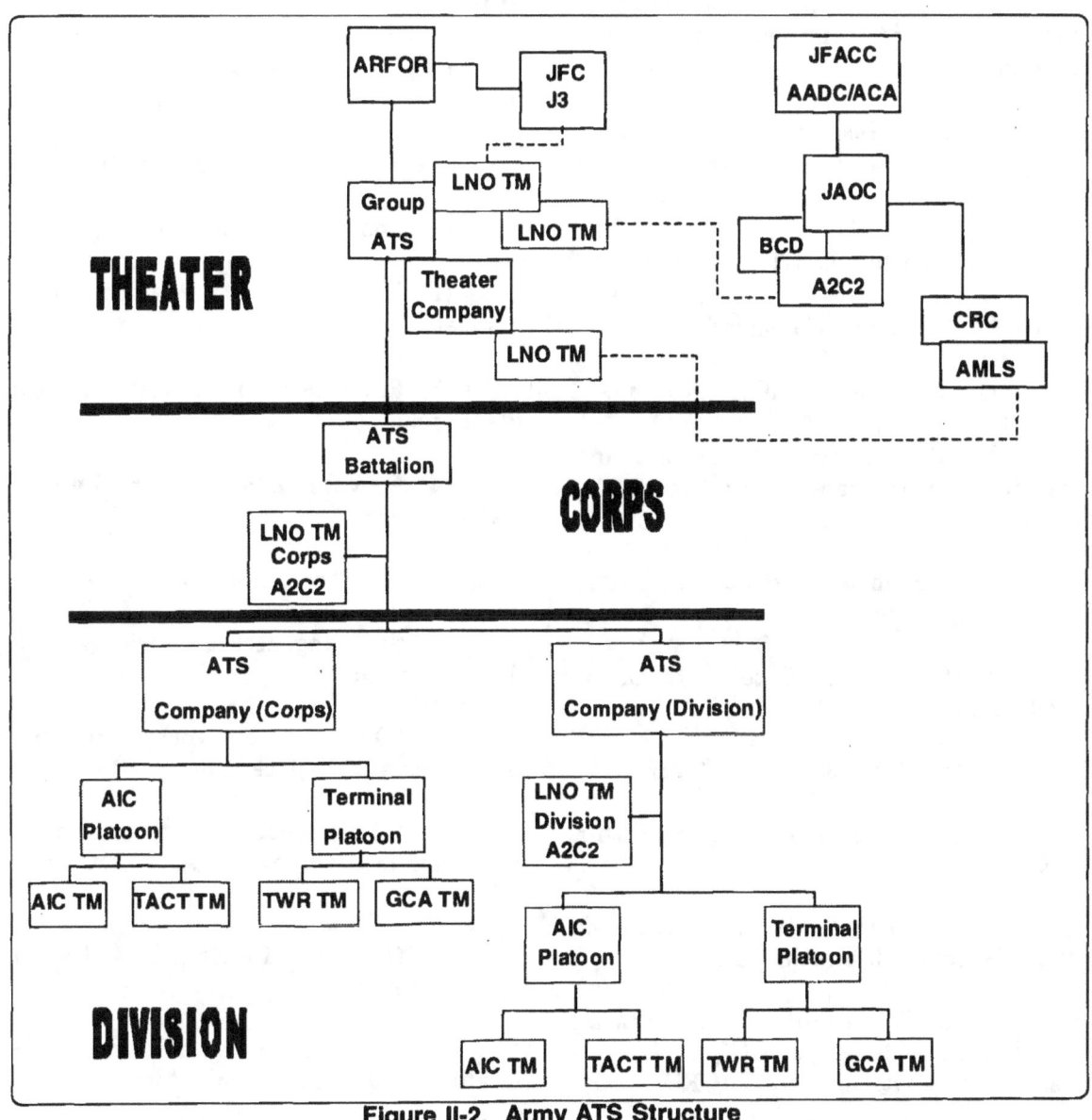

Figure II-2. Army ATS Structure

(b) LNO Team to BCD/JAOC.

•Represents US Army air traffic interest to BCD for inclusion in ACP and resultant ACO/SPINS.

•Continuous coordination of US Army airspace control measures (ACMs).

•Provides input to ACP development.

(c) LNO team (provided by theater support company) to CRC.

•Provides representation/coordination with USAF airspace management element.

•Provides linkage to AICs airspace and air traffic management elements.

•Coordinates ATC procedures.

b. ATS Battalion Commander.

(1) Commands the ATS battalion.

(2) Advises corps/division commanders on airspace/air traffic implementation/employment.

(3) Implements corps/division commanders guidance.

(4) Provides LNO team to Corps A2C2 element.

(a) Responsible to G-3 Air.

(b) Integrates activities within A2C2 element.

(c) Deconflicts, synchronizes, and integrates all airspace users.

(d) Represents air traffic requirements to corps, BCD/AOC, and control and reporting center (CRC).

(5) Publishes APG for JOA.

(6) Provides quality assurance (QA) for ATS ratings, standard, procedures, TERPS, and training.

(7) Reviews and forwards TERPS developed by subordinate elements through A2C2 elements to AOC for integration in joint procedures.

(8) Trains battalion on ATS collective tasks.

(9) Disseminates ACP and ACO/SPINs as required.

(10) Coordinates US Army ATS locations, capabilities, and status.

c. ATS Company Commander (USA).

(1) Commands company.

(2) Implements battalion commander's guidance.

(3) Provides inputs to corps/division planning.

(4) Provides LNO team to division A2C2 element.

(a) Responsible to G-3 Air.

(b) Integrates activities within A2C2 element.

(c) Deconflicts, synchronizes, and integrates all airspace users.

(d) Represents air traffic requirements to corps, BCD/AOC, and CRC.

(e) Disseminates ACP and ACO/SPINs as required.

(f) Coordinates US Army ATS locations, capabilities, and status.

(5) Provides ATS liaison to division A2C2 element.

(6) Trains company on ATS collective tasks.

(a) Installs ATS equipment.

(b) Operates ATS equipment.

(c) Maintains ATS equipment.

d. Facility Chief (Controller).

(1) Develops facility training manual guidance in FM 1-303.

(2) Supervises training and mission execution of individual ATS tasks.

(3) Installs particular pieces of ATS equipment (that is, tower, GCA [ASR/PAR] radar, AICs, and nondirectional beacons [NDBs]).

(4) Operates equipment stated above.

(5) Develops TERPS for GCA/NDB approaches.

(6) Coordinates maintenance of above stated equipment.

e. Controller (USA).

(1) Installs ATS equipment.

(2) Operates ATS equipment.

(3) Maintains ATS equipment.

(4) Controls all types of air traffic.

f. Airspace Management Liaison Section (AMLS). AMLSs are established at appropriate elements within the ACS and are manned by Army personnel along with representatives from other components involved to include allied representation. The AMLS coordinates the operational

commander's airspace requirements and requests the establishment of special procedures for airspace use. These sections also assist the ACA in coordinating and integrating flight operations and air warning information of the components (FM 1-303).

g. BCD. The BCD is an Army liaison provided by the Army component commander to the AOC and/or to the component designated by the JFC to plan, coordinate, and deconflict air operations. The BCD processes Army requests for tactical air support, monitors and interprets the land battle situation for the JAOC, and provides the necessary interface for exchange of current intelligence and operational data (Joint Publication 1-02).

4. Navy and Marine Corps ATC Duties, Responsibilities, and C2 Relationships

a. Introduction. C2 of Navy/Marine Corps ATC assets and personnel will be closely related to the C2 structure for airspace control. As such, decision making, asset allocation, and implementation will flow through the existing airspace control infrastructure. Additionally, in most operations the amount of land based Navy/Marine Corps ATC, relative to the other Services will be smaller with the preponderance of assets and effort sea-based. Once the Marines are established ashore, ATC operations will be a subset of the existing airspace control organization and will rely on that organization for communications and coordination.

b. Sea-Based. For the Navy, ATC facilities (sea-based) are resident in the specific platforms that are capable of launching and recovering aircraft. The two biggest platforms being the aircraft carrier and the "large deck" amphibious assault carrier. These two platforms form the preponderance of sea-based ATC. There are smaller ships that launch and recover aircraft; however, their capabilities are generally restricted to terminal approach and landing on their specific platform. Sea-based airspace control nodes are built around sensor assets and capabilities including the ability to receive and transmit data. These are also centered on the larger ships in the battle group; however, most of the other ships can provide information via data link to these larger ships.

c. Navy Tactical Air Control System (TACS).

Figure II-3 illustrates the Navy TACS. This is the primary airspace control and communications structure designed as warfighting entities. *Note: Not shown in the diagram and illustrated below are two key links that join Navy sea-based airspace control and coordination (warfighting) with sea-based ATC entities:*

Carrier. Composite Warfare Commander (CWC)—CVBG/CDC—CATCC.

Amphibious. CWC—TACC/CDC—AOCC.

(Warfighting/Airspace Control)—ATC coordination.

Because of these key links, any ATC coordination and control can utilize the same channels of communication within a JTF that the warfighting C2 utilizes.

Navy or Marine Corps issues relative to ATC can flow up and down the same existing chain of command that accommodates issues relative to warfighting within the JTF.

d. Marine Air Command and Control System (MACCS). Figure II-4 illustrates the MACCS. The MACCS gives the ACE commander the ability to exercise

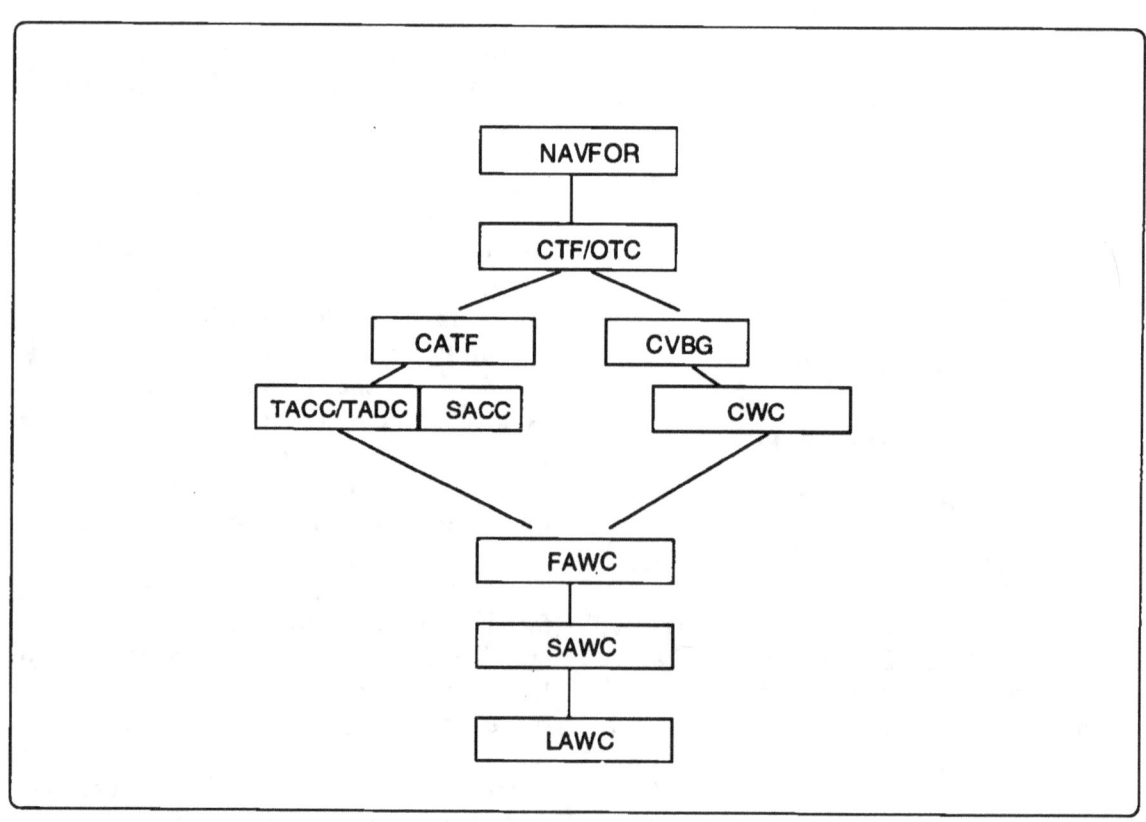

Figure II-3. Navy TACS

centralized command and coordination and decentralized control of MAGTF air assets and operations. The MACCS allows interface of MAGTF air with joint or combined operations. The MACCS is an air C2 system, which provides the ACE commander the means to command, coordinate, and control all air operations within an assigned sector as directed by the JFC. It allows the ACE commander to coordinate air operations with other Services. It is made up of C2 agencies with communications-electronics equipment that includes manual through semiautomatic control capability. The MACG of the MAW has the personnel and equipment required to establish the bulk

of the MACCS. The mission of the MACG is to provide, operate, and maintain the major elements of the MACCS.

e. LNOs. One of the most important elements of both airspace control and the ATC link is the various LNOs provided to the JAOC and other key organizations. In accordance with JFACC/AADC/ACA directives, LNOs at the JAOC will affect the largest portion of the control and coordination relative to Navy and Marine Corps ATC issues. As issues come up the chain of command (warfighting), the LNO has the ability to coordinate ATC issues directly with the airspace control cell within the JAOC.

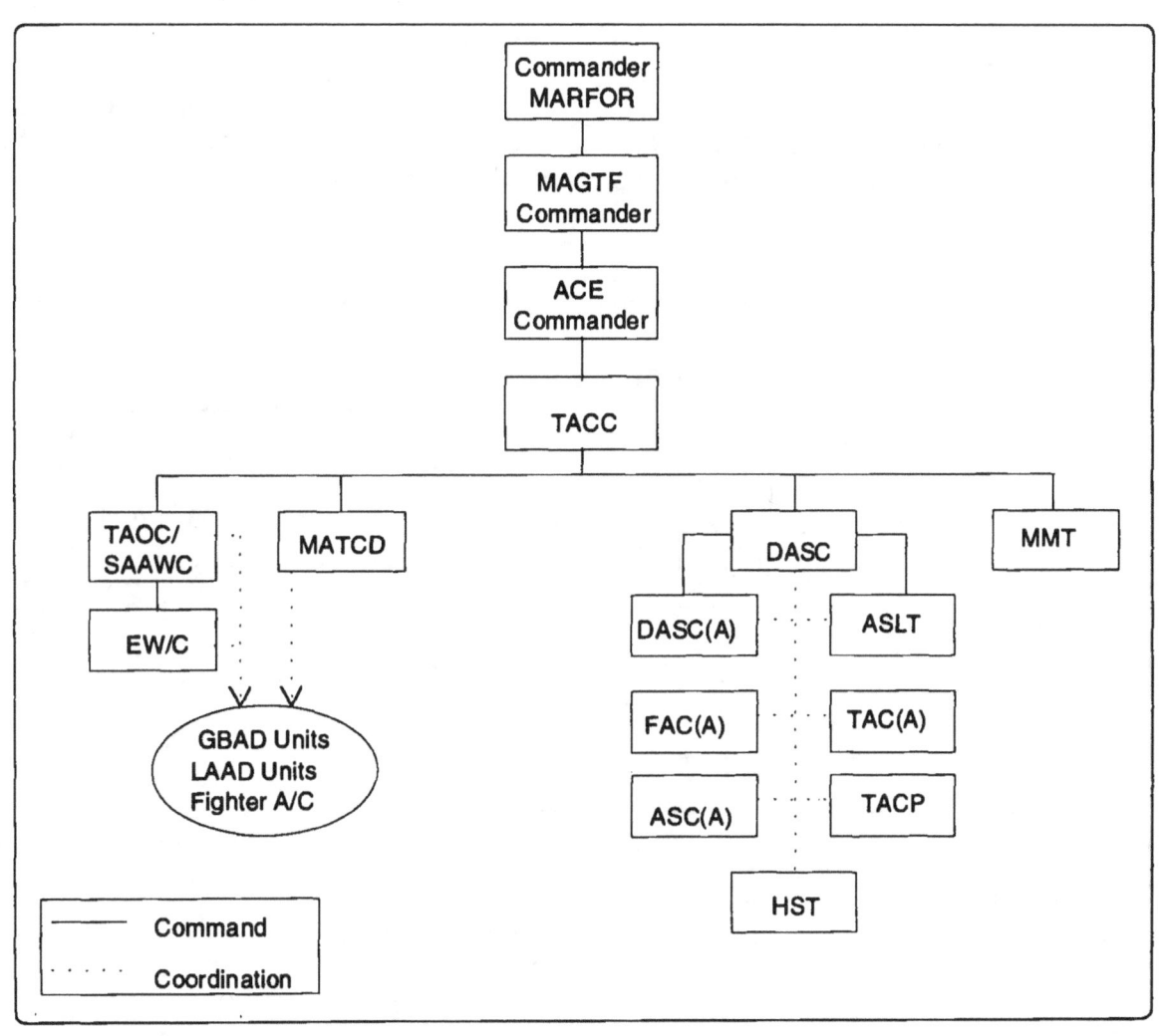

Figure II-4. MACCS

5. Air Force ATC Duties, Responsibilities, and C2 Relationships

The USAF ATC system provides service and coordination from CONUS, through en route locations and international airspace, to the beddown locations for combat aircraft, to aerial ports of debarkation, to forward-deployed austere airfields, and return. While combat and force enhancement aircraft (all Services) usually conduct a singular deployment/ redeployment to the theater, ongoing passenger (flown by both Civilian Reserve Air Fleet [CRAF] and military aircraft) and cargo flights comprise the steady stream transcontinental air traffic. Therefore, the USAF focuses on both the en route and distant end deployed ATC service. See Figure II-5 for the AF ATC structure.

a. En Route Support.

Experience in deploying large numbers of military aircraft necessitated providing liaison to the FAA and host nation ATC systems. The USAF has liaisons in all the FAA regions and a central contingency cell at the flow control office in Washington Center, Reston, Virginia. Part of their function is to ensure enough FAA controllers are available to meet unusual military traffic loads.

Additionally, the USAF has ATC liaisons in several foreign ATC facilities to assist host nation controllers in understanding of US military aircraft requirements/procedures. These locations currently include Paris, France; Moron Air Base, Spain; and Fairford Air Base, and Uxbridge Air Base, England. Additionally, the USAF has ATC liaison packages that can be assigned to host nation ATC facilities and US Embassies. These liaisons coordinate with the deployed US ATC units, the JAOC, the host nation ATC system, the US Embassy, the USAF Air Mobility Command's Tactical Air Control Center, and other ATC liaisons to deconflict air flow problems.

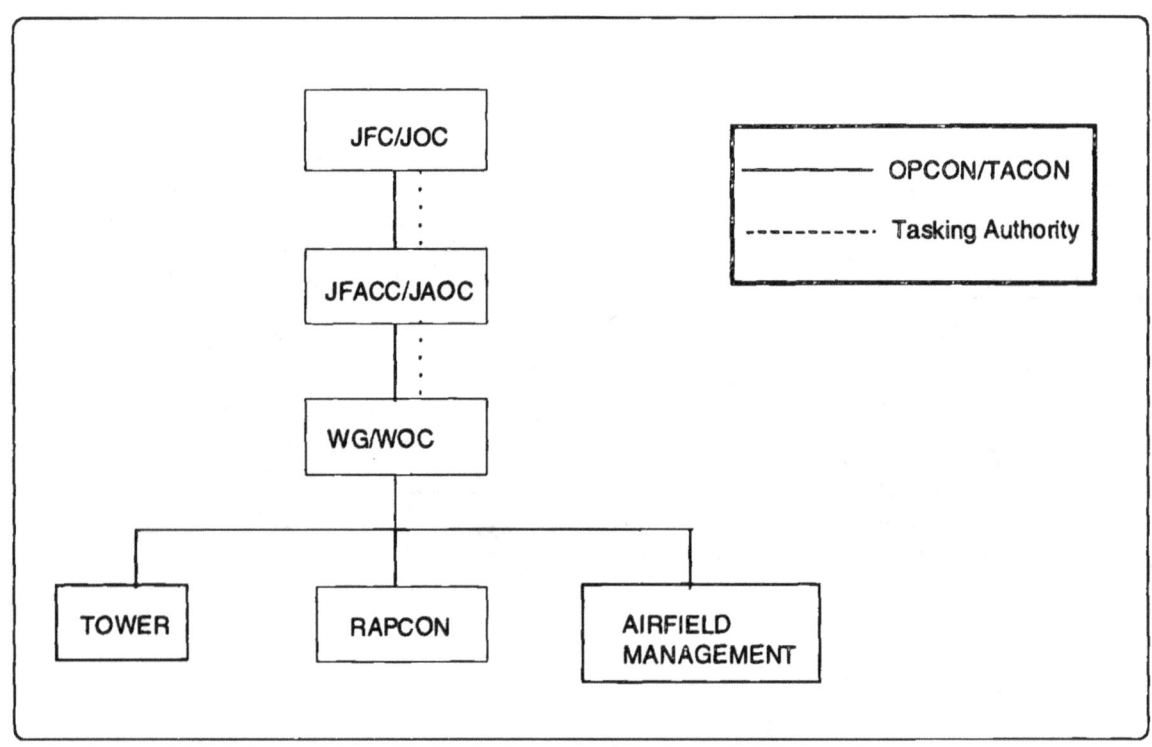

Figure II-5. Air Force ATC Structure

b. Deployed Terminal Locations.

At the deployed base, the senior AF ATC representative, normally the airfield operations flight commander (AOF/CC), will coordinate—

(1) Terminal instrument procedure and flight check support.

(2) Any change in airfield status immediately with the JAOC.

(3) Host nation/airspace for international diplomatic clearance.

(4) Terminal area operation procedures with the base defense operations center for integration into the base air defense and air base ground defense plans and operations.

(5) Integration into the TACS IAW JAOC guidance contained in the Tactical Operational Data (TACOPDAT) and OPTASK link messages via the ACP.

(6) With the host service for host-provided base operating support (BOS) to include billeting and messing facilities, fuel, power production, vehicle support, secure communications, and security.

AF ATC is aligned primarily within the wing operations center (WOC). These assets are theater based.

Generally, in a combat theater/AOR, air traffic and airspace C2 systems are integrated under a single combined/joint forces ACA. Since ATC units are subordinate to the WOC, their facilities and personnel (fixed, tactical, and augmented), in some theaters, become a part of the Theater Air Control System (TACS). It is only through this relationship that they are considered part of the TACS. Controllers perform terminal air traffic operations or liaison/augmentation at host nation control facilities. ATC planning, training, and operating procedures must reflect this

concept and any additional mission/roles, prioritized in the Defense Planning Guidance to include support for two major regional contingencies (MRCs); MOOTW such as humanitarian relief and disaster response; operational readiness inspections; and test or demonstrations.

c. ST. One of the keys to successful air/ground operations requires timely, detailed planning involving air forces, ground users, and ST forces. Planning for ST operations should begin early in the crisis action planning cycle. During situation development and crisis assessment, the theater special operations command (SOC) ST planner should be assessing the situation to determine possible ST missions, identifying key planners for coordination for future course of action (COA) development, and verifying the availability and status of theater ST assets. Normally the 720th Special Tactics Group (STG), Hurlburt Field, Florida, will be included in the coordination through AFSOC channels providing planning inputs (and planners if available) and assessment of the possible need for CONUS augmentation. Requirements for ST planners and LNOs are mission dependent with the exception of specific requirements in the JAOC, joint special operations air component (JSOAC), and JRCC. The ST planner must be prepared to respond to evolving ST support requirements spanning minor conflict, MOOTW, and MRCs, normally as part of a joint or coalition force. The Chairman of the Joint Chiefs of Staff (CJCS) Warning Order initiates COA development and the ST planner must be prepared to meet the needs of multiple planning agencies and LNO from the theater SOC down to the supported unit level. During this phase, time-phased force and deployment data (TPFDD) refinement should begin through logistics (J-4) channels to begin identifying/refining forces, transportation requirements, and shortfalls. As mentioned earlier, ST forces will normally plan, deploy/employ, and operate as part of a joint/

combined force. STTs usually deploy to the intermediate staging base (ISB) for joint employment into the AO or target area; however, units may employ directly from home station if required. Once employed, ST ATC operations will focus on target assessment (airfield, DZ, CAS/artillery target), establishing C2, NAVAIDS emplacement/sitting, and then on terminal guidance for airlift or CAS operations including deconflicting lethal fires within their assigned airspace. Since SOF operations usually occur beyond the ground commanders deep battlespace, the use of ACM is critical to protect SOF assets including restricted operating zones (ROZ) and no fire areas (NFAs). SOF ACMs must be reflected in the ACO. Units should forward requests for specific ACMs through unit channels to the ACA for consideration and inclusion into the ACO. Operations within the close, deep, or rear areas will also require coordination through the ACO including links to adjacent facilities, JSOAC/TALCE, elements of the TACS, and

fire direction/control functions. Precision approach capability involves siting the MMLS (TRN-45), TACAN (TRN-41), runway lighting package, completing a TERPS site survey, and obtaining certification or authorization for air assets to fly the approach. STTs are capable of completing all siting tasks except the certification which requires specialized aircraft to flight check the system or command review and risk assessment to accept the approach. Finally since ST forces are lightly armed, they are dependent on the TACON unit for security. Logistics, with the exception of meals and water (Class I), is a component responsibility including ammunitions, petroleum, oil, lubricants (POL), communications, NAVAIDS, employment systems, and maintenance (Class III, V, VII, IX). ST sustainment operations are heavily dependent on resupply to replenish consumables, especially batteries for communications/NAVAIDS systems. See Figure II-6 for the ST C2 structure.

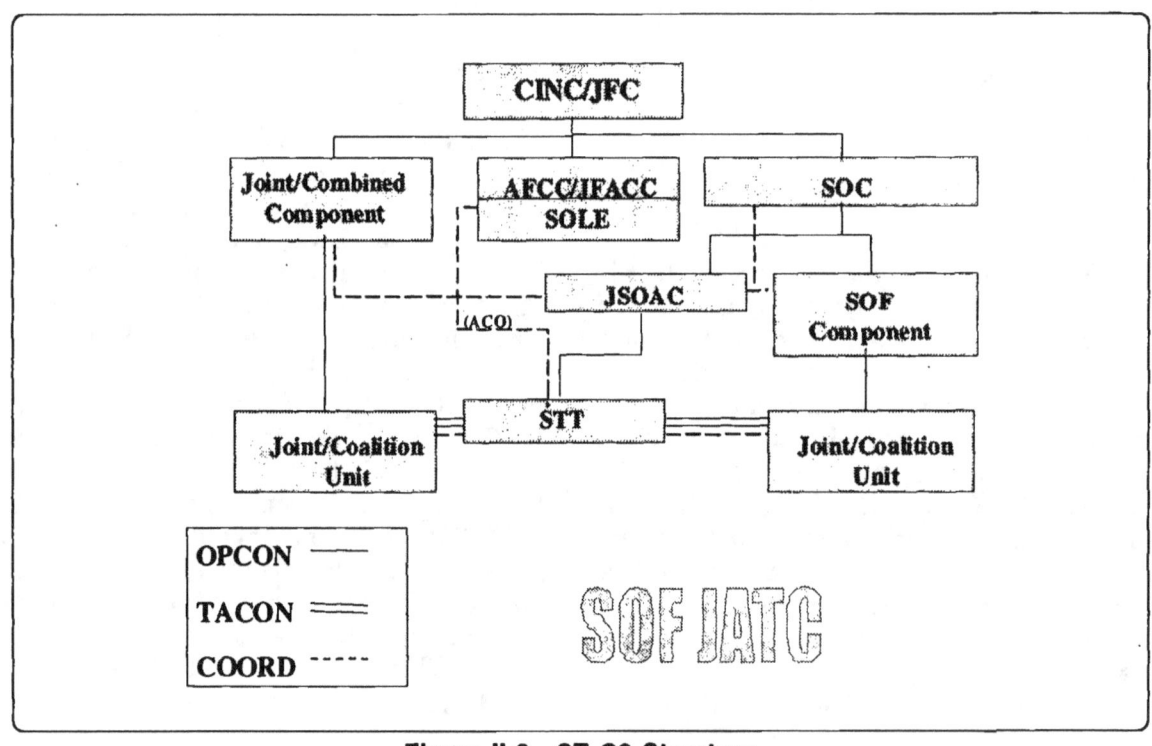

Figure II-6. ST C2 Structure

6. Joint ATC Force Deployment and Employment

a. Background.

A joint force planner must understand and integrate the elements of each Service's ATC capabilities to effectively support the JFC's requirements. To be capable of executing this responsibility requires a general understanding of how these forces fit in the flow of a developing theater and a general understanding of employment capabilities. See Table E-3 for information on ATC communications capabilities.

Each Service effectively plans, deploys, and force protects their aviation/airspace control personnel and DATCALS in support of their own operations. In a joint environment, each Service has different capabilities to employ ATS assets from initial to sustained operations based on the requirements of their specific aircraft and missions. The Army maintains light, highly mobile systems, forces for early entry and ATS capability to sustain and manage airspace within the Army's AOR. The Army can provide ATS support of joint operations by providing task organized assets that supplement or augment the other Services (that is, highly mobile radar systems, qualified controllers, long range mobile tactical airspace communication systems). Their integration is most effective in the initial phase of an operation and through transition until a sustained capability can be employed. The Marines are self-sustaining, highly mobile, and organized to execute their primary mission, supporting MAGTF operations, and are also capable of supporting joint operations up to a full-up fixed base-like airfield. The Navy is robust and fleet based but has limited capability to support a land based ATC structure. The AF covers a wide spectrum of ATC capabilities from an initial first entry tactical ATC, utilizing STTs, to a full-up, fixed base-like airfield environment.

Historically the initial phase of employing ATS resources for the JFC, the AF or Army ATC has entered the AOR to establish the initial ATC capability. However, depending on the scenario, the Marines might also be the first and only Service to establish initial land based ATC operations. In this phase, it is crucial for a joint planner to know the condition and capabilities of airfield, NAVAIDS, and other airspace management resources in the AOR. This will dictate the type and mix of assets required to support airland operations until a full AF or Marine sustainment package can be deployed. If forced entry is the preferred option, it will require a specific mix of forces and a determination by the JFCs of the levels of risk that they will accept to accomplish this objectives. Chapter III addresses how the Service specific resources can be integrated through each phase to effectively and efficiently use them to support a JTF commander.

In the sustainment phase of the operation as the AOR matures, the AF can provide full theater air base (TAB) sustaining ATC packages, and the Marines can provide full-up IFR airfield ATC capabilities.

To effect C2 of ATC operations through all phases, the JFC has to determine the priority of personnel and equipment that is required in the AOR and has to have a clear chain of responsibility for implementation of the decisions. The JFACC, when appointed, exercises the planning, coordinating, and directing of air and space operations to support the JFC's decisions through the JAOC. The JAOC is the senior operations center and focal point for air and space operations planning and execution. Each theater may have unique processes driven by coalition/allied interoperability, but the majority of JAOC processes are standard. The JAOC director is charged with the effectiveness of joint air and space operations and focuses on planning, coordinating, allocating, tasking, executing, and assessing air and space power operations in the AOR/JOA based on JFACC guidance. The director of combat plans (DCP) is directly responsible to the JAOC director for planning and allocating forces IAW guidance issued by JFC and JFACC. The airspace management and control team is under the direct control of the DCP. It is the single theater focal point responsible for developing and coordinating airspace control measures. Airspace managers monitor the status of airfields, NAVAIDS, and TACS facilities for impact on planning and developing an ACO, which includes all airspace control measures. Component or functional command liaisons operate in the airspace management and control team assisting in the integration and coordination of their specific organization's ATC employment and airspace requirements. It is essential that they are included in planning for each phase and have communication connectivity with their organizations. Additional responsibilities of airspace management and control team personnel include—

(1) Assigning control areas in coordination with the JTF/combined tasked force (CTF) and host nation.

(2) Tailoring DATCALS and AO packages to meet specific mission needs (every attempt should be made to keep the package as small as possible).

(3) Working with the component staffs and/or liaison officers (ARFOR, NAVFOR, MARFOR, AFFOR, and SOC) to coordinate the movement/replacement of the STT with general purpose ATC.

(4) Developing airspace control procedures that are simple and flexible with minimal reliance on voice communications.

(5) Developing flow control procedures that readily allow EMCON operations.

(6) Coordinating terminal control procedures with each base/airfield operations and/or host nation base

operations authority. Include surge launch and recovery procedures.

(7) Coordinating airspace control procedures with air base ground defense and air defense procedures.

(8) Ensuring airspace control procedures comply with published rules of engagement.

(9) Scheduling and coordinating flight inspection requirements with the FAA flight inspections or theater FAA liaison assigned to the JAOC.

(10) Developing guidance for employment addressing waivers to separation standards, ATO versus flight plan filing and ATC radar performance of air defense surveillance functions.

b. Considerations for the Joint Planner. In the preplanning or in the initial process of implementing the JTF commander's decisions, the following are considerations for the joint planner:

(1) Initial Operations. An initial deployment assessment, preferably on the terrain, must be conducted. Then a determination of force mix must be made. Minimal airfield operations services should be provided until sustaining DATCALS arrive. Small, lightweight, minimum capability and highly mobile packages will provide initial VFR or limited (procedural control rather than positive control) IFR ATC. Airborne deployed fighting forces and supporting units deploying in initial phases of a crisis should be self-sufficient (that is, food, water, shelter, etc.) for up to 72 hours. After this time, the ATC forces will require resupply and/or augmentation UTCs to continue operations. These assets may or may not remain at the location after initial deployment airflow is complete.

This phase would normally end with a sustainment airfield capability to effect further airflow or airlanded capability. The joint planner must consider resources to support a transition period if sustainment assets are not available to relieve the initial deployment capability. Higher priority forces may delay the arrival of sustainment ATC assets. Reliance on the initially deployed ATC assets reduces the throughput capability of an airfield until the more robust sustainment package arrives in theater. The paradox is that the equipment required for providing full IFR capability is airlift-intensive.

(2) Sustainment Operations. Sustaining deployment will provide airfield operations to supplement the initial deployment phase and provide required positive control IFR capability up to dual runway precision approach. This will provide full base airfield operations support for an extended period of time. A full range of terminal (mobile control tower, ASR, precision landing capabilities, and/or navigational aids both space- and ground-based) and transmission medium equipment is included in this phase. Airfield management augmentation personnel from CONUS bases are required for this phase.

(3) Additional Considerations. For the joint planner additional considerations include development of an IFR capability, establishing different levels of capability based on the level of acceptable risk, and establishing a rotation and redeployment plan to sustain the operations. More detailed discussion of critical areas follows:

(a) TERPS. Survey qualified (SST and selected ACC) TERPS specialists conduct/participate in initial site surveys. All TERPS specialists use this information to develop approach procedure packages and forward them to the MAJCOM TERPS office responsible for the designated AOR. When required, MAJCOMs may delegate final review and approval authority to wing and group level or combat communications units to support unique geographical requirements for short-notice deployments. When delegating review and approval authority (standard procedures) forward a copy of the correspondence to the

supporting MAJCOMs and Air Force Flight Standards Agency (AFFSA). All non-standard procedures will be processed through MAJCOMs, IAW AFMAN 11-230 and AFM 11-206. Authorization to use the procedures ultimately remains with the appropriate MAJCOM flying operations authority and/or the commander exercising operational control of the aircraft. During contingency operations, the AF component commander may request the establishment of an in-theater TERPS cell for the purpose of developing and approving instrument procedures and scheduling flight inspections. While STT and deployed ATC units have some organic TERPS capability, Pacific Air Forces (PACAF), United States Air Forces Europe (USAFE), ACC, and Air Mobility Command (AMC) have TERPS cells which can provide technical assistance in developing and reviewing instrument procedures. TERPS cells will review requested airfield locations that USAF aircraft plan on using during IMC. ACC is developing a deployable TERPS capability to conduct such surveys and review.

(b) Flight Inspection. These flights certify instrument procedures and their associated NAVAIDS for use under IFR. As such, flight inspection has both operational and legal ramifications. The following four options reflect the different degrees of flight inspection available to the Theater CINC or JFC (listed from higher to lower risk). *Note: Options 1 and 2 are available in cases where a flight inspection is impossible/limited and military operations must be conducted. However, Options 1 and 2 do not eliminate the __requirement__ to conduct a flight inspection before IFR use. The flight inspection requirement is postponed until the situation permits inspection IAW Options 3 or 4.*

•Option 1. Commander's Decision. Commanders have the final authority and responsibility for accomplishing their assigned mission. If the military situation dictates, the theater commander may approve the use of a navigational aid/

approach without a flight inspection (see Note on page II-15, 6b[3][b]). This can be approved only for military aircraft under the operational control. Other aircraft (FAA/CRAF/ICAO, etc.) are normally not authorized to use the facility.

•Option 2. Military Emergency Use Only. The commander may approve abbreviated flight inspection procedures/ profiles using a military aircraft if necessary (requires visual meteorological condition [VMC] weather). This normally takes ½ day and 1 sortie to complete. This option is intended to permit a commander to continue flight operations while waiting for a restricted or normal commissioning inspection (see Note on page II-15, 6b[3][b]). This inspection will allow a theater commander to have temporary IFR capability for "MILITARY AIRCRAFT ONLY." Other aircraft (FAA/CRAF/ICAO, etc.) are normally not authorized to use this facility.

•Option 3. Restricted Facility Commissioning. This inspection certifies the facility for IFR approach use only. Optimally it will take 1 day and 2 sorties (VMC weather) to complete. This inspection permits DOD, CRAF, FAA, and ICAO aircraft use. Areas that are evaluated acceptable are certified, the rest of the areas/procedures are restricted. The local (deployed) airfield operations/air traffic control manager will publish the restrictions in appropriate Notices to Airmen (NOTAM).

•Option 4. Normal Commissioning. This is the certification of all procedures (arrival/approach/ departure) and areas of NAVAIDS coverage. Optimally this inspection takes 2-3 days and 4-5 sorties (VMC weather) to complete. This inspection is required for full use by DOD, CRAF, FAA, and ICAO aircraft.

(c) Flight Inspection Beddown. FAA supplies civilian maintenance personnel and mobility readiness spares package (MRSP) equipment for operations. For contingency operations, aircraft maintenance support should to be located outside hostile areas with an optimum bed-down location within 300 miles of airfields to be flight inspected. For theater operations, the FAA will establish a maintenance base with deployed MRSP and aircraft maintenance personnel (civilian) in or near the AOR. This includes one pilot in the AOC used for ATO coordination. The requesting ATC representative must provide approach procedures packages and specific airfield site survey data to flight inspection aircrews and the flight inspection liaison assigned to the JAOC, before flight inspection can begin.

(d) Distribution of Approaches. The AOR TERPS office completes the TERPS database using survey information and develops an approach procedure. The developed approach procedure is transmitted to the airfield for flyability check/flight inspection as required. Based on results of flyability check/flight inspection and theater commander's approval, the AOR TERPS office disseminates the completed procedure(s) to theater aircrews, Headquarters (HQ) AMC TERPS office, and HQ AMC TACC for distribution to AMC aircrews. *Note: Procedures developed by the AOR TERPS office only apply to aircraft within the theater (after theater commander approval) until an FAA flight inspection can be accomplished (see AFMAN 11-225, Section 109, for flight inspection requirements).*

(e) Redeployment. DATCALS are theater assets. When the individual AF units rotates out of theater, DATCALS equipment will remain in place. By leaving the DATCALS equipment, repetitive airlift and flight inspection requirements are reduced.

(f) Personnel Rotation. As the theater matures and airlift becomes available, it may become necessary to rotate personnel. PALACE MANNING programs

(Blitz, Tenure, etc.) run by AF Personnel Center in conjunction with supporting MAJCOMs IAW AFI 10-215, are the primary method for rotating AF personnel. MAJCOM airfield operations functional managers should work closely with their personnel community to assist/recommend units/volunteers for the tasking. UTC rotation is the secondary method to support deployed airfield operations. The supported MAJCOM or NAF planners will determine if rotations are sourced using either PALACE or UTC programs. The initial rotation should be staggered so all personnel do not rotate at the same time to allow for training/spin-up time for replacements.

(g) Planning Factors.

•Combat attrition factor will be a minimum of three bare bases or as specified in the current defense planning guidance.

•Language speaking requirements will be requested through the PALACE BLITZ program and not identified as an UTC requirement.

•A site survey/advanced echelon (ADVON) team of personnel, to include a TERPS qualified controller, should deploy a few days ahead of the equipment in order to determine siting location and special requirements for connectivity.

•ANG will use volunteers to the maximum extent possible. When volunteers are no longer viable, active duty may assume responsibility for manning the location or ANG unit may be activated using Presidential Selective Reserve Call-up (PSRC), IAW AFI 10-402. During initial planning ensure this option is available.

•Communications Connectivity (see Table E-3).

•Once the JTF commander's plan has been developed and promulgated by the ACP/ACO or orders to the component/functional commanders, the liaison elements and the component/functional command staffs must plan and coordinate their execution of the JTF plan. The liaison elements are essential to keeping this effort integrated and coordinated across each Service.

(h) Long Term Support. At the 120-day demarcation, regardless of tasked unit(s), planners should initiate requests with the supported CINC or JTF to consider installation or lease of semipermanent DATCALS to replace limited deployable wartime assets.

(i) Strategic Transportation. The process and procedures for strategic transportation of JATC requirements are contained in Joint Publication 4-01, *Joint Doctrine for the Defense Transportation System*.

Chapter III

PLANNING CONSIDERATIONS FOR INITIAL, TRANSITION, AND SUSTAINED JATC OPERATIONS

1. Background

The primary planning factors for any contingency should be environment, time, and required capabilities. Planners for joint/combined operations need to evaluate the ATC support requirements (personnel and equipment) for each operating location in terms of airfield purpose/permanence, speed of deployment, immediate operational capability, aircraft type/mix, and ultimate level of capability.

With these planning factors in mind, this chapter outlines the initiation, transition, and sustainment of JATC operations. It provides methods to integrate, synchronize, and possibly provide interoperability with each Service's ATC systems. Refer to Appendix E for a complete listing of Service specific equipment and capabilities.

To effectively execute these complex operations, planners must recognize how critical selection of forces is to the success of the operation. ATC personnel may be functioning from airfields that include joint, allied, and civil aircraft. The airfield may have virtually no infrastructure. These personnel must be versatile, intimately familiar, and experienced with their own capabilities and trained in joint/ multinational ATC and airfield operating procedures in order to effectively enhance aircrew safety and mission success. In an environment where facilities may support host nation, combined forces, or a high volume of mixed traffic including rotary-wing aircraft, the importance of dedicated ATC liaison personnel cannot be overstated. Consideration of establishing joint/ combined teams at facilities that draws on the specialized skills and experience of each member is paramount to safe and efficient operations.

Figures III-1 through III-3 and accompanying text provide a scenario outline and specific considerations to assist joint planners in understanding the chapter discussion.

2. Initial Operations

For the purposes of this publication and the scenario, initial entry is defined as military actions required to airland forces with inter or intratheater airlift to meet the JFC's strategic or operational objectives. Initial entry starts with deployment of ATC assets in an opposed or unopposed entry. This could be accomplished through use of surface, amphibious, airborne, airland, or heliborne operations. See Figure III-1.

a. Special Tactics Team.

Although all Services are capable of providing an initial ATC capability, AF ST teams are uniquely trained and specifically equipped to provide initial airfield operations for inter and intratheater airlift in a joint environment. USAF ST could be augmented by another Service's initial ATC capability depending on the method of insertion and type of aircraft in the airflow. For example, AF ST can be inserted by any method. AF airlift and special operations require ST capability. Marine MMT and Army TACT are more limited. Marine MMT and Army TACT can only be used if Marine or Army aviation is a major component of the airflow. In this scenario, IFR weather conditions at the objective area restrict the method of entry to an airborne operation.

The airborne combat or security forces would come from the Army; however, the only ATC element currently capable of providing both airborne personnel and air-droppable ATC landing systems are USAF ST Teams.

ST forces will be organized under the OPCON of the SOC or TACON to the theater air component. When these forces are air dropped into the objective area, security forces will secure the area and the STT will initiate the setup of the communications, runway lighting system, TACAN, and MMLS and initiate the TERPS process for the landing zone. To complete the process of preparing for air operations, the responsible authority must determine the acceptable level of risk. Once the STT establishes the airfield and the ground forces commander determines the area is relatively secure, airland operations may begin. Refer to Table III-1 for initial entry planning considerations. Incorporation of special operations aircraft, such as Combat Talon, with specialized navigation and night vision equipment can effectively extend the range of options addressed in the scenario to put an initial ATC capability in place.

INITIAL

OBJECTIVE: Establish airfield operations for strategic and theater airlift under IFR conditions.

ATC SERVICES/ACTIONS	D-72 to 12HRS	H HOUR	1 HRS	TBD	5 HRS	5-12 HRS	12-24 HRS	24 HRS	48 HRS	72 HRS
ST FORCES ALERTED	X									
GATHER INTEL	X									
ST FORCES DEPLOY/EMPLOY		X								
AIRFIELD SIEZURE (AIRBORNE INSERTION)		X								
AIRFIELD ASSESSMENT, COMM ESTABLISHED			X							
MARKING/LIGHTS, BEACON, & TACAN OPERATIONAL			X							
AIRFIELD READY TO RECIEVE TRAFFIC			X#							
AIRFIELD SECURE W/LIGHT HOSTILITIES				X^						
INITIAL DAY/NIGHT VFR ATC BEGINS				X@						
AIRLAND ADDITIONAL ST FORCES/EQUIPMENT					X					
AIRLAND ADDITIONAL GROUND FORCES/EQUIPMENT					X	X	X	X	X	X
MMLS OPERATIONAL						X				
TERPS INFORMATION FORWARDED							X			
MMLS FLIGHT CHECKED							X*	X*	X*	
AMC TALCE ARRIVES								X		
AMC TALCE OPERATIONAL								X		
MMLS APPROACH APPROVED							X*	X*	X*	X*
LIMITED IFR SERVICES AVAILABLE							X*	X*	X*	X*

\# Special Tactics Team Leader (STTL) determination

^Ground Forces Commander (GFC) Determination

@ Joint Determination by STTL, GFC, and Air Mission Commander

*JFC risk acceptance approval, flyability check, or FAA Flight Check required

Figure III-1. Initial Planning Considerations

Transition to
SUSTAINMENT

OBJECTIVE: ST relieved, more robust systems in place from Air Force, Army or Marine tactical ATC units.

TIME LINE	3-5 DAYS	7 DAYS	10 DAYS	14 DAYS	21-25 DAYS	30 DAYS	45+ DAYS
SUSTAINMENT ATC FORCES/EQUIPMENT ARRIVES	X	X					
USAF COMBAT COMMUNICATIONS							
ARMY ATC							
MARINE ATC							
TRANSITIONAL ATC BEGINS			X	X			
TERPS APPROVED/PUBLISHED					X		
SUSTAINMENT MMLS OPERATIONAL					X		
GCA OPERATIONAL					X		
PAR OPERATIONAL					X		
PAR/GCA APPROACHES APPROVED							
ST HANDS OFF ATC TO SUSTAINMENT FORCES					X		
SUSTAINMENT ATC ASSUMES RESPONSIBILITY					X		
ST FORCES REDEPLOY WITH ALL ST EQUIPMENT						X	
HOST NATION RESUMES ATC SERVICES							X
SUSTAINMMENT ATC REDEPLOYS							X

Figure III-2. Transition to Sustainment

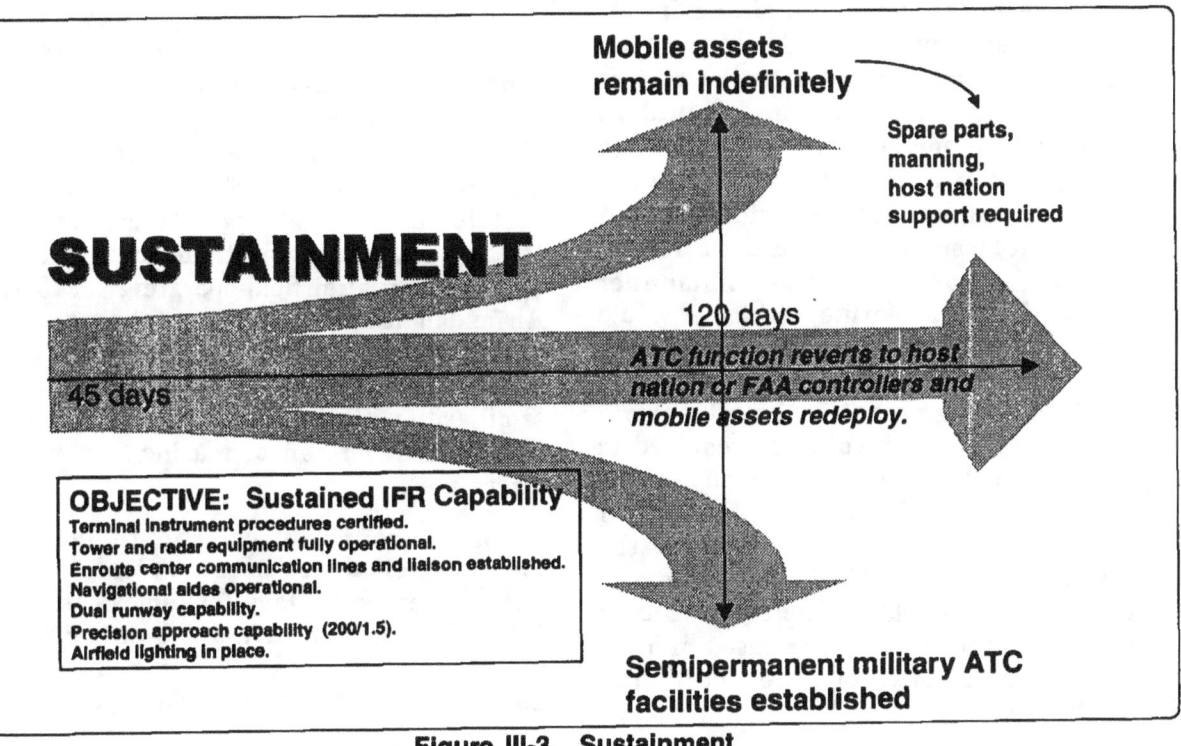

Mobile assets remain indefinitely

Spare parts, manning, host nation support required

SUSTAINMENT

120 days
ATC function reverts to host nation or FAA controllers and mobile assets redeploy.

45 days

OBJECTIVE: Sustained IFR Capability
Terminal instrument procedures certified.
Tower and radar equipment fully operational.
Enroute center communication lines and liaison established.
Navigational aides operational.
Dual runway capability.
Precision approach capability (200/1.5).
Airfield lighting in place.

Semipermanent military ATC facilities established

Figure III-3. Sustainment

Table III-1. Initial JATC Capabilities

Service	Voice Communication			Deployable NAVAIDS	Runway Lighting	Visual Flight Rules (VFR)	Limited Instrument Flight Rules (IFR)
	VHF (Secure)	UHF (Secure)	FM (Secure)				
USA	No	Yes	Yes	NDB	No	Yes	No
USAF	Yes	Yes	Yes	MMLS	Yes	Yes	Yes
USMC	Yes	Yes	No	MRAALS	Yes	Yes	Yes

b. Navy. During the initial phase, Navy TACRON controllers perform their duties aboard the amphibious flagship for operations in direct support of amphibious task force operations. They are responsible for providing centralized command, control, planning, and coordination of all air support and airspace required for amphibious operations. This control continues until control is passed ashore to the DASC. TACRONs maintain the capability to temporarily staff and operate an existing ATC facility ashore or augment, with personnel, a remote facility ashore to control air traffic during the sustainment phase.

c. USMC. While Marine ATC forces normally establish airfields and provide ATC operations for Marine aircraft, they have the capability of providing initial entry forces to support establishing a joint LZ. These forces are restricted to surface or heliborne operations and would be inserted with one helicopter that could fly into the objective area supported by security forces and under weather conditions that provide at least "see and avoid" conditions. Under the control of the commander landing force, the Marine ATC forces would then initiate the setup of an MMLS and the LZ in the same manner as the STT. Additional augmentation by ST TERPS qualified personnel would be required to establish airfield markings and approaches for AF aircraft. Flight verification and or flight check requirements would be the same. Initial entry Marine ATC forces in this scenario would be limited to LZs in proximity to the littoral area based on flight time limitations of the heliborne platform(s).

d. Army. Army ATC forces could be integrated into either the initial entry forces or during the transition period, based on special requirements in the initial entry or based on the need to prepare for forward deployment of Army forces arriving after the LZ is established. An Army TACT could airdrop into the objective area with the STT and simultaneously assist in the TERPS and establishment of the landing zone. The Army alone could not provide a limited IFR airfield capability for other Service's aircraft without significant resourcing from another Service for equipment such as runway lighting and airfield marking. The Army can establish an instrumented airfield limited to rotary-wing operations with organic equipment.

e. General Capabilities. All Services have initial ATC radio communications capability. Initial landing systems are more limited, being matched to very specific aircraft systems such as the TACAN, Marines ARA-63 airborne radar, or AF MLS. The Marines and AF ST have packable/portable airfield lighting systems organic to their units allowing them to provide a complete initial airfield-operating package. Airfield lighting and marking patterns need to be coordinated to determine if the initial entry force has the equipment and familiarity with the marking patterns used by AF airlift aircraft or Marine fixed-wing aircraft.

Subsequent replacement, replenishment, or augmentation must occur within approximately 14 days for almost all the initial forces identified. Contingency planners must program this transition package carefully because deployment of the sustainment ATC forces for both the AF and Marines require significant airlift assets and may not be prioritized in the air flow. For example, if initial entry forces need airport surveillance or precision approach radar early in the entry, the Army approach radar system is the most compact and capable of early deployment. Army ATC forces are capable of full tower, surveillance/approach radar, and flight following central AIC operations.

3. Transition Operations

Transition operations are defined as operations during the period where the initial entry ATC resources require replacement, replenishment, augmentation, or upgrade of ATC services until sustainment ATC forces are established. For planning purposes, this could be for an extended period of time based on the intended time frame of the operation or availability of airlift or sealift resources to deploy sustainment ATC forces. Planners should consider initial entry might meet the desired operational capability. However, USAF ST will need relief to reconstitute the initial entry capability and provide a more conventional airfield environment. For example, the ST battery operated lighting systems will need to be replaced with less expensive but bulkier generator powered airfield lighting that will provide more than emergency lighting levels. Under ideal conditions, operations will flow from initial to sustained, without the need for a distinct transition force (Figure III-2). Transition operations require handover procedures to transfer control of operations from one ATC service provider to another. See Appendix I for sample handover checklists.

The following planning considerations, required to bridge the gap between the initial entry force and the sustaining force, are built around a worst case, medium threat, IFR scenario. For discussion purposes, the initial entry force has conducted a forced entry, secured and established a single, hard surfaced runway with a requirement to establish a precision approach to accommodate rotary-wing and up to heavy airlift aircraft. The objective is to eventually land strategic airlift aircraft, (including the C-17 Globemaster III) and conduct transition operations to handover to sustainment forces. The strategic and operational objective necessitates a high risk to be assumed. Therefore, the JFC has authorized use of the LZ without any flight validation or certification. The risk is significant but operations still require a validation for the approach. This will be accomplished utilizing a Combat Talon, MC-130 aircraft, to execute a flyability check and subsequently validate the procedure (in lieu of, an FAA flight check that is only conducted under day, VFR, nonopposed conditions). The approach could then be flown by all Services' aircraft with JFC approval. This does not eliminate the requirement for a flight inspection. See Chapter II, Section 6b(3)(b).

All possible contingencies could not be incorporated into the above scenario. Some additional issues to consider when resourcing a transition force can be found in Figure III-4 and Table III-2.

The ability to synchronize ATC resources and activities in time and space to produce maximum operational effectiveness requires special attention to individual Service capabilities and limitations. STTs require relief, resupply or replenishment not later than (NLT) L+14. These forces are normally unable to conduct extended handover operations based on higher HQ tasking to move forward. Transition forces must be capable of short duration handovers (24-48 hours) to relieve ST forces. Army TACTs are normally also unable to conduct extended handover operations and require resupply or relief NLT L+72. As discussed in initial entry, USMC ATC forces are limited to LZs in proximity to the littoral area based on flight time limitations of their airborne platforms.

PLANNER'S TRANSITION CHECKLIST

ISSUES TO CONSIDER WHEN SOURCING A TRANSITION FORCE

- Mission.   Airflow: aircraft type/volume/type of ATC service.
- Environment.   Hostile/nonhostile base support/terrain/weather.
- Time (i.e., airlift). How long is the transition gap/how long to get in place?
- TACS Interface.
- Transfer.
- Handoff template.
- Key contacts (maintenance, communications, weather, etc.).
- Procedures (ATC, air defense, etc.).
- Airspace.
- Communications capability.
- Coordination requirements/procedures with adjacent facilities.
- Base support.
- Rules of engagement.
- Equipment left behinh—who will maintain?
- What equipment is compatible/incompatible?
- Overlap, continuity of service.

Figure III-4. Planner's Transition Checklist

Table III-2. Transition and Sustainment Operations

Transition and Sustainment JATC Operations					
Service/System	Approach	GCA	Tower	Limitations	Remarks
USA		X	X	See FM 24-24	Transition/Sustain
USAF/ANG	X	X	X	See AFI 13-220	Sustain
USMC	X	X	X	See MCWP 3-25.8	Transition/Sustain

Integration and interoperability of ATC systems is highly complex and may require extensive research into equipment capabilities and support requirements. Service systems are designed as stand-alone with some limited connectivity. Planners must first identify what systems are in place and what systems are required. The key to solving integration and interoperability issues lie with the subject matter experts in each Service. Appendix E includes a limited description of each Service's equipment

The initial entry force may be composed of USAF STT, USA TACT, or USMC MMT forces. This force has established a form of landing capability that will eventually have to be replaced or upgraded. Based on the traffic density, type aircraft, weather, terrain, and duration of support, the joint planner needs to refer to Table III-2 to determine what assets best fill the gap between initial and sustainment forces.

4. Sustainment Operations

Sustainment operations exist when ATC forces have achieved desired operational capability and conclude when long term facilities are constructed or redeployment occurs. To establish a sustainment ATC capability requires significant planning to ensure appropriate airlift capability is available and the flow meets the JFC's requirements. Establishment of a sustainment airfield provides the capability for full IFR support of military and civil aircraft. FAA certified ILS approach capability would be necessary to effectively integrate CRAF support of deployment operations.

All Services can provide sustained capability for both VFR and IFR service to all Service aircraft through mobile control towers, radar systems, and communications connectivity. The Army system is only limited by the extent they can be resupplied/maintained. Navy shipboard systems are only limited by the ability of the ship to remain on station and maintain its systems operational. AF and Marine sustaining equipment is extremely robust and requires extensive airlift to deploy but provides complete ATC service to support a theater airbase mission. See Figure III-3.

a. Synchronization. The planning considerations for a transition phase are the same as for the sustainment phase. Equipment availability is only one of the major planning factors in determining the "end result" capability. Logistical support for equipment is a driving consideration. Replacement parts and trained maintenance technicians are Service and often equipment specific. In a few systems (for example, TSW-7 ATC Towers), the Services share the same ATC equipment and could be left in place, reducing airlift requirements. In any case, base support (power, communications, supply, and personnel) needs to be in place to support sustained ATC operations. Depending on the equipment deployed, setup time will vary from hours to 2 days (in good weather conditions) and then requires a complete flight check. Therefore, flight operations requiring a sustained ATC ability should be planned no sooner than 3 days after equipment arrival.

b. Integration. Determination of the base's purpose drives the need for integration. If the base is strictly a single Service location (for example, an USA helicopter base or an USAF cargo/fighter base), then integration may not be a consideration. However, if multiservice flight operations will occur, appropriate Service ATC liaisons should augment the ATC facilities. While English is one of the international flight languages, consideration for including a foreign language qualified individual might be required to work host nation/ATC issues.

c. Interoperability. Current combat ATC systems are designed with Service specific requirements and are not specifically set up to interoperate with other Services. In addition, direct links and procedures do not exist to connect tactical air control systems with USAF tactical ATC systems. Finally, due to distinct differences between aircraft performance and procedures, planners should request controllers experienced/current with anticipated traffic.

5. End of Operations

The end of the sustainment would occur by either redeployment of the equipment, installation of permanent equipment, or transfer to the host nation air traffic control system. Drawdown of operations may require reversing the buildup process and necessitate the second deployment of initial entry (for example, STT) assets who are able to operate without base support. End of operations will require a handover or phaseout of ATC services. See Appendix I for sample handover checklists. The deployed equipment may be redeployed to another location, returned for maintenance, or even transferred to the host nation as part of the foreign military sales program.

Appendix A

AIR TRAFFIC CONTROL FORCE STRUCTURE

1. Background

This appendix outlines the deployable air traffic control (ATC) force structure in the Services.

2. Army Air Traffic Services (ATSs)

For active duty ATS tactical units, 45 percent of their strength is in CONUS; 27.5 percent of the strength is in Europe; and another 27.5 percent is in the Pacific. Table A-1 outlines the Army ATC tactical units.

3. Marine Air Control Squadrons (MACSs)

There are 5 active duty and 2 reserve MACSs. The active duty MACSs are located at—

- Marine Corps Air Station (MCAS) Cherry Point, North Carolina.

- MCAS Beaufort, South Carolina.

- MCAS Yuma, Arizona.

- MCB Camp Pendleton, California.

- MCAS Futenma, Okinawa, Japan.

Note: The MACSs at Cherry Point and Beaufort will be consolidated into a single squadron in the near future. Similarly, the MACSs at Pendleton and Yuma will be consolidated into 1 squadron. Each consolidated squadron will contain 4 Marine ATC detachments (MATCDs).

The reserve MACSs are based out of Damneck, Virginia, and Aurora, Colorado. The reserve MACS in Damneck has 2 MATCDs. The reserve MACS in Aurora does not have any MATCDs. The MATCDs are positioned to support MCASs throughout CONUS and Western Pacific (WESTPAC).

The MATCDs of each MACS are located at—

- MACS-1 ATC Det A, MCAS Camp Pendleton, California.

- MACS-1 ATC Det B, MCAS Tustin, California.

- MACS-2 ATC Det A, MCAS Beaufort, South Carolina.

- MACS-2 ATC Det B, MCAS New River, North Carolina.

- MACS-4 ATC Det A, MCAS Futenma, Okinawa, Japan.

- MACS-4 ATC Det B, MCAS Iwakuni, Japan.

- MACS-6 ATC Det A, Marine Corps Auxiliary Landing Field, Bogue, North Carolina.

- MACS-6 ATC Det B, Marine Corps Auxiliary Landing Field, Bogue, North Carolina.

- MACS-7 ATC Det A, MCAS Yuma, Arizona

- MACS-7 ATC Det B, MCAS El Toro, California.

- MACS-24 ATC Det A, Naval Air Station (NAS) Joint Reserve Base, Fort Worth, Texas (Reserve).

- MACS-24 ATC Det B, NAS Joint Reserve Base, Willow Grove, Pennsylvania (Reserve).

Table A-1. Army ATC Force Structure

UNIT	TYPE	SUPPORTING	ALIGN	LOCATION
29th ATS Gp (NG)	EAC Gp	3d Army/USAREUR	SWA	Glen Arm, MD
164th ATS Gp	EAC Gp	8th Army	NEA	Seoul, KOR
1-58th Bn	Corps Bn	XVIII Corps	XVIII Corps	Ft Bragg, NC
A/1-58 ATS	Corps Co	XVIII Corps	XVIII Corps	Ft Bragg, NC
B/1-58 ATS	Abn Div Co	82 Abn Div	XVIII Corps	Ft Bragg, NC
C/1-58 ATS	AAslt Div Co	101st AA Div	XVIII Corps	Ft Campbell, KY
D/1-58 ATS	Div Co	3 Mech Div	XVIII Corps	Ft Stewart, GA
E/1-58 ATS	Div Co	10th LID	XVIII Corps	Ft Drum, NY
F/1-58 ATS	Div Co	1st Cav Div	XVIII Corps	Ft Hood, TX
3-58th Bn	Corps Bn	V Corps/USAREUR	V Corps	Wiesbaden, GE
E/58 ATS	EAC Co	USAREUR	NATO	Sandhofen, GE
C/3-58 ATS	Corps Co	3-58th Bn	V Corps	Wiesbaden, GE
A/3-58 ATS	Div Co	1st Arm Div	V Corps	Hanau, GE
B/3-58 ATS	Div Co	1st Mech Div	V Corps	Ansbach, GE
2-114 Bn (NG)	Corps Bn	III Corps	III Corps	Little Rock, AR
E/111 ATS (NG)	EAC Co	3d Army	SWA	Jacksonville, FL
D/114 ATS (NG)	Corps Co	2-114 Bn (NG)	III Corps	Little Rock, AR
232 ATS (NG)	Div Co	III Corps	4th Mech Div	Jackson, MS
1-103 Bn (NG)	Corps Bn	I Corps	I Corps	Ft Lewis, WA
B/4-58 ATS	EAC Co	8th Army	NEA	Uijonbu, KOR
145 ATS (NG)	Corps Co	I Corps	I Corps	Lexington, OK
A/4-58 ATS	Div Co	2d Mech Div	I Corps	Camp Casey, KOR
G/58 ATS	Div Co	25th ID	I Corps	Schofield Bks, HI
H/104 ATS (NG)	Div Co	28th Arm Div	I Corps	Harrisburg, PA
G/238 ATS (NG)	Div Co	38th Mech Div	I Corps	Shelbyville, IN
49 ATS (NG)	Div Co	49th Arm Div	I Corps	San Antonio, TX
129 ATS (NG)	Div Co	29th Inf Div	I Corps	Edgewood, MD
181 ATS (NG)	Div Co	34th Div	I Corps	Bangor, MN
416 ATS (NG)	Div Co	40th Mech Div	I Corps	Phoenix, AZ
426 ATS (NG)	Div Co	42d Div	I Corps	Camp Edward, MA
670 ATS (NG)	Div Co	35th Div	I Corps	Smyrna, TN
F/58th ATS	Maintenance	All ATS units	Worldwide	Ft. Rucker, AL

4. Navy Tactical Air Control Groups (TACGRUs)

a. TACGRU 1 is located at Naval Amphibious Base (NAB) Coronado, San Diego, California. Its subordinate units are tactical air control squadrons (TACRONs). TACRONs 11 and 12 are squadrons under Group 1. The TACRONs deploy as detachments throughout the Pacific Fleet AOR to provide centralized planning, control, and integration of all air operations in support of amphibious operations.

b. TACGRU 2 is located at NAB Little Creek, Norfolk, Virginia. Its subordinate units are TACRONs. TACRONs 21 and 22 are squadrons under Group 2. The TACRONs deploy as detachments throughout the Atlantic Fleet AOR to provide centralized planning, control, and integration of all air operations in support of amphibious operations.

5. Air Force Providers

The Air Force has 16 deployable air traffic control and landing systems (DATCALS). Three systems are located at the 3rd Combat Communications Group, Tinker Air Force Base (AFB), Oklahoma. Three systems are maintained at the 5th Combat Communications Group, Robins AFB, Georgia. Both combat communications groups include a limited number of air traffic controllers within the DATCALS packages. Ten systems are located at the ANG ATC squadrons across the country and include a full package of controllers and maintainers. The remaining ATC personnel are dispersed across various units, to include AFSOC special tactics squadrons, active duty combat ATC units and DATCALS-augmentees from CONUS-based MAJCOM operations support squadrons. MAJCOMs with a capability to provide augmentee controllers are listed in Table A-2.

Table A-2. Air Force ATC Providers

MAJCOM
Air Combat Command (ACC)
Air Mobility Command (AMC)
Air Force Materiel Command (AFMC)
Air Education and Training Command (AETC)
Air Force Special Operations Component (AFSOC)
Air National Guard (ANG)

Notes:

　　a. **Special Tactics Teams (STTs).** *The special tactics structure is organized into the 720 Special Tactics Group (STG) Group, Hurlburt Field, Florida. Under the 720 STG are the 21 Special Tactics Squadron (STS), Pope AFB, North Carolina; the 22 STS, McChord AFB, Washington; the 23 STS, Hurlburt Field, Florida; the 24 STS, Ft Bragg, North Carolina; the 320 STS, Kadena, Japan, (Operational Control [OPCON] to the 353 Special Operations Group [SOG]); the 321 STS, Mildenhall, England (OPCON to 352 SOG, and an Operating Loation-A (OL-A) with liaison officers at HQ AMC, Scott AFB, Illinois. The 720 STG gains the 123 Special Tactics Facility (STF) at Louisville, Kentucky, ANG 2.*

　　b. ANG Air Traffic Control Squadrons are structured and organized under the host base wing commander, with the exception of—

　　(1) The 297 Air Traffic Control Squadron, Barbers Point, Hawaii, that is aligned under the 201 Combat Communications Group (CCG) that in turn is aligned under the 154 Fighter Wing (FW), Hickam AFB, Hawaii.

　　(2) The 259 Air Traffic Control Squadron, Alexandria, Louisiana, is aligned under the 159 FW, Louisiana.

　　(3) The 235 Air Traffic Control Squadron, Selfridge ANGB, Michigan, is aligned under the 127 FW, Michigan.

　　(4) The 248 Air Traffic Control Squadron, Meridian, Mississippi, is aligned under the 186 Air Reconnaissance Wing (ARW), Mississippi.

　　(5) The 258 Air Traffic Control Squadron, Johnstown, Pennsylvania, is aligned under the 193 Special Operations Wing (SOW), Pennsylvania.

　　(6) The 241 Air Traffic Control Squadrons, St. Joseph, Missouri, is aligned under the 139 Air Wing (AW), Missouri.

　　(7) The 245 Air Traffic Control Squadrons, McEntiree Air National Guard Base (ANGB), South Carolina, is aligned under the 169 FW, South Carolina.

　　(8) The 243 Air Traffic Control Squadron, Cheyenne, Wyoming, is aligned under the 153 AW, Wyoming.

　　(9) The 260 Air Traffic Control Squadron, Pease International Tradeport, New Hampshire, is aligned under the 157 ARW, New Hampshire.

　　(10) The 270 Air Traffic Control Squadron, Klamath Falls IAP, Oregon, is aligned under the 173 FW, Oregon.

SERVICE COMPONENT CAPABILITIES MATRIX

Air Traffic Control Capabilities	TERPS Site Survey	TERPS	Airfield Survey[3]	Day VFR[4]	Night VFR[5]	Tactical Airfield Lighting	Limited IFR Services[6]	Full IFR Services[7]	Precision Approach Radar	Airfield Management	Flight Check
Air Force Combat Communications	X[1]	X[1]		X	X[12]		X	X	X[8]	X[13]	X[15]
Fixed Base[10]		X		X	X		X	X	X	X	X[15]
Air Force Special Tactics Teams (STT)	X[1]		X[2]	X	X[11]	X	X	X		X	
Air Guard	X[1]	X[1]		X	X[12]		X	X	X[8]	X	
Army	X	X	X[14]	X	X		X	X	X		X[16]
Army Guard				X	X		X	X	X		
Marine Corps	X1	X[1]	X[2]	X	X	X	X	X	X		
Navy				X[3]	X[3]		X[3]	X[3]	X[3]	X	

1. TERPS specialists (USAF Special Experience Identifier 361) should also be used to conduct site surveys. If possible, utilize the same personnel for the survey and to build the approaches.
2. Basic airfield survey done during initial entry phase. Not a formal site survey that may be used to gather data for TERPS certified approaches.
3. Navy AOCCs aboard LHA/LHD class ships primarily provide ATC services to aircraft in support of the amphibious task force and have the capability to provide approach control services to land-based satellite airports. TACRONs are capable of temporarily staffing (or augmenting) and operating shore-based ATC facilities.
4. May be anything from one person with a portable radio to a MRC-144 communications vehicle to an entire mobile tower package.
5. Airfield lighting or aircrew NVG systems required.
6. Limited to TACAN, NDB, or MMLS systems. No approach control or precision approach functions.
7. May be limited to nonradar operations that may hamper operational tempo.
8. USAF PAR controllers require Special Experience Identifier 365 and must be tasked accordingly to ensure qualified controllers are deployed.
9. USAF airfield management personnel are tasked by the same command authority as ATC personnel. Navy controllers are qualified in both specialties.
10. Fixed base UTCs consist of personnel only that normally join with USAF Combat Communications equipment in the forward area or may be tailored (TPFDD) to work in host nation or interservice facilities.
11. STT carry their own airfield lighting. (All others require tactical lighting systems or operational host-nation systems).
12. Requires tactical lighting systems or operational host-nation systems.
13. Airfield management services at austere locations may be provided by AMC Tanker-Airlift Control Element (TALCE).
14. Generally limited to helicopter operations.
15. USAF members work with and are tasked through FAA.
16. Single C-12 operation for USA requirements.

TRAINING AND PERSONNEL COMPARISONS

	Army	Air Force (Conventional ATC)	Air Force (Special Tactics Combat Control)	Navy	Marine Corps
Initial ATC Training Location/Duration	Ft Rucker, AL, 11 Weeks	Keesler AFB, MS, 15 weeks	Combat Control ATC Center Keesler AFB, MS, 15 weeks Combat Control Indoctrination US Army Airborne Parachutists Course Combat Diver Qualification Course Combat Survival Training Course Underwater Egress Military Freefall Parachutist Course Combat Control Apprentice Course	Pensacola NAS, FL, 14 weeks	Pensacola NAS, FL, 14 weeks
Job Specialties Awarded	93C10	1C1XX	J1C2XX	AC1-3/ACC ACCS/M	ACA1/A2/A3
Advanced Training			Combat Control Craftsman Course Survey and Assault Zone Assessment Course Automated TERPS Tactical Radar Approach Control Various advanced parachuting, diving/amphibious, survival, tactical leadership, and contingency planning courses		
Other Courses	Pathfinder School Airborne School Air Assault AGOS[2] JFCC JAOSC Battle Staff Course NCO Crs TERPS[3]	Combat Control Apprentice Course ATC Craftsman Airfield Management Apprentice/Craftsman Military Airspace Management TERPS	Joint Air Operations Staff Course Joint Firepower Control Course Naval Gunfire Spotters Course Naval Tac Air Control Party USMC TACP	Carrier ATC Ops Course Amphibious ATC Ops Course Advanced Radar Air Traffic Control	MATCALS[1] Operators Course Advanced MATCALS Advanced Radar Air Traffic Control Weapons and Tactics Course Weapons and Tactics Instructor Course

Career Progression	Army	Air Force (Conventional ATC)	Air Force (Special Tactics Combat Control)	Navy	Marine Corps
	Apprentice (E1-E4)	Controller (E1-E4)	Apprentice (E1-E3)	Apprentice (E1-E5)	Apprentice (E1-E5)
	Controller in Charge (E4-E5)	Watch Supervisor (E5-E6)	Journeyman/AZ Controller (E3-E4)	Journeyman (E5-E6)	Watch Sup Crew Chief (E5-E7)
	Shift Supervisor (E5-E6)	Chief Controller, Facility Chief (E7-E9)	Craftsman /LZSO (E5-E6)	Senior Controller (E7-E9)	Tower/Radar Chief (E6-E7)
	Facility Chief (E6-E7)	AOF/CC CATCOs(ANG) (O1-O4)	Superintendent/Manager (E7-E9)	Lead Chief (E8-E9)	NCOIC (E7-E8)
	ATC Chief (E7-E8)	ATCS/CC (ANG) (0-5)	Flight Commander/Team Leader (O1-O3)		
	Platoon SGT (E7)				
Force Strength					
Military-Active (RC)	Enlisted – 1032 (1034)	Officer -203 Auth Enlisted 3138 Auth	Officer - 60 Auth Enlisted 425 Auth	Officer-65 Enlisted-2534	[4] Officer-100 Enlisted-650
Civilian[5]	303	Not Available	0	40	0

1 Marine Air Traffic Control and Landing Systems
2 AGOS is a multiservice school
3 USAF/FAA
4 RC strength not available
5 Civilian Job Classification (2152)

Appendix D

ARMY AIR TRAFFIC SERVICES TASK-ORGANIZED ELEMENTS

1. Background

This appendix lists and describes the primary task-organized elements in Army ATS.

2. Tactical Aviation Control Team (TACT)

TACTs are employed at auxiliary areas and remote locations. TACTs can provide Army aviation units with on-the-spot control and advisory capabilities in any environment. The TACT provides terminal control and advisory services at any location where Army aviation requires coordinated movement of aircraft. They can be organized in several configurations using an easy to pack secure data/voice communications package. TACTs are task organized to support specific missions in the forward areas. The focus is always on providing support to aviation; the goal is to ensure coordinated aviation operations at austere landing areas. With its secure, long range communications, the TACT is ideal for providing terminal area services at remote, austere landing areas. TACT operations will provide portable, lightweight NAVAIDS for passage points and landing site designation and integration. The mobility of the TACT allows the commander flexibility during all stages of force projection. The TACT can perform short-term independent operations (for not more than 72 hours). Most tailored force packages using aviation assets should include TACTs.

3. Tower Teams

Tower teams are normally employed at main operating bases where high-density air traffic exists. This team provides tower services similar to those that are conducted in a fixed base environment. Tower teams

control air traffic that is transitioning, landing, or departing main operating bases or tactical landing sites. The tower team is the primary ATS organization for regulating and integrating ATS terminal services at the main operating base. It also establishes the nonprecision approach capability for the terminal area of operations. All aircraft movements at the airfield or tactical landing site that the aviation operations section or appropriate Army airspace command and control (A2C2) element initiates should be coordinated with the tower team. Tower teams and TACTs can use NVDs to detect threat air and ground forces during offensive or defensive operations.

4. Ground Controlled Approach (GCA) Team

The GCA team normally employs with the tower team at main operating bases. This team provides a near all-weather, precision, and nonprecision approach and recovery capability. It also provides surveillance vectoring and precision/nonprecision approach guidance to arriving and departing aircraft operating in the terminal area.

5. A2C2 Liaison Element

Airspace management doctrine requires that A2C2 liaison elements be assigned at all echelons from brigade to EAC. The A2C2 liaison team furnishes the personnel for the A2C2 elements at each echelon. It provides A2C2, airspace information, and air traffic services integration. The liaison teams are the primary players in helping A2C2 cells provide synchronization, regulation, identification, and deconfliction of all airspace users. These teams must be robust enough to afford 24-hour services yet mobile enough to move rapidly as combat operations develop.

6. Communications Zone (COMMZ) Support Company

The COMMZ support company can provide teams to support terminal area operations at up to 4 designated airfield locations or austere landing sites in the theater. These locations are expected to be used for sustainment operations where joint and multinational forces aircraft conduct landings and takeoffs. The company can move rapidly using its internal TACTs in a terminal configuration.

7. Corps Support Company

The corps support company provides a terminal team to support terminal area operations at each designated airfield or austere landing site. It also provides airspace information services in the corps area of operations. The company can move rapidly using its internal TACTs in a terminal configuration.

8. Division Support Company

The division support company provides—

a. Two TACTs.

b. Airspace information services in the division area of operations.

c. The division maneuver brigade's A2C2 elements with A2C2 liaison personnel.

d. Terminal area services at each designated airfield location or austere landing site.

e. The division airspace information center (DAIC), which is organic to the division support company and collocated with the division A2C2 cell.

9. Assault Division Support Company

The assault division support company is the same as the division support company except for the number of TACTs. The company provides—

a. Six TACTs.

b. Airspace information services in the division area of operations.

c. The assault division maneuver brigade's A2C2 elements with A2C2 liaison personnel.

d. Terminal area services at each designated airfield location or austere landing site.

e. The division airspace information center, which is organic to the assault division support company.

10. Corps Airspace Information Center (CAIC)

The CAIC is the primary ATS facility that provides A2C2 services, airspace information services, and coordination of Army, joint, and multinational air traffic operating in the rear operations areas. It is also the primary interface with the joint and multinational airspace management system concerning the coordination of flights conducted within the LCC AOR. The CAIC provides—

a. Updates that include hostile aircraft intrusion warnings.

b. On-call demand activated NAVAIDS, dissemination of terminal airfield status.

c. Flight following and navigational assistance.

d. Aircraft sequencing on designated flight routes.

e. Assistance in defensive and offensive operations.

f. Dissemination of current and forecasted aviation weather information.

g. Search and rescue assistance to aircraft performing CSAR operations.

h. The collection, processing, displaying, and dissemination of critical A2C2 information.

11. Division Airspace Information Center (DAIC)

The DAIC provides A2C2 information and is employed in the division area of operations. The DAIC supports the CAIC with its coordination activities. The DAIC also can provide real-time air picture situational updates as required. The DAIC relays current and forecasted weather information and is the primary coordination link between the brigade A2C2 and division A2C2 cells. Although located at different echelons, all airspace information centers (AICs) perform essentially the same function and have the same tactical equipment. When the CAIC is inoperative or moving, the ATS commander will designate another AIC to serve as the main AIC. The redesignated AIC operates and employs the same as the original CAIC. This link ensures continuity in the flow of information required for air defense and air traffic management operations.

AIR TRAFFIC CONTROL EQUIPMENT

1. Background

This appendix contains a list and description of the most common ATC equipment used by the Services.

2. Army ATC Equipment

a. ATC Facility-AN/TSQ-97.

(1) Description. The AN/TSQ-97 is a portable ATC facility for control of air traffic at landing zones (LZs) in forward areas. It can also be used at any LZ where visual flight rules (VFR) control is required. Included in the facility are the following radio communication capabilities: 1 ultra high frequency (UHF) radio, 1 very high frequency (VHF) radio, and 1 frequency modulation (FM) radio.

(2) Installation. This equipment is not actually installed as such, but is set up for use where needed. When employed at an airfield, it is only utilized temporarily until larger and more capable facilities are installed. The facility can be set up and operational in about 10 minutes.

(3) Operation. The AN/TSQ-97 can be operated in the normal manner during periods of rain, if suitable waterproof covering is used to shield the facility from direct drenching. This facility, however, will not be operated during electrical storms. When the battery has been cycled under moderate to warm climatic conditions, it should not be used in extreme cold as cells may crack. When relocating to cold environments, new batteries should be used. Three air traffic controllers are required for the AN/TSQ-97.

(4) Interface. The AN/TSQ-97 can interface with other deployed communications facilities via field phones or UHF/VHF/FM radio. Cables are supplied to interface security equipment for X-mode (secure) communications. The AN/TSQ-97 has no integral landline communications console. The TSQ-97 uses analog equipment for communications and requires special consideration when interfacing with digital equipment.

(5) Transportation Requirements. The facility with batteries weighs about 200 pounds and is intended to be personnel-transportable for short distances.

(a) By ground: 4 soldiers.

(b) By road: any cargo carrying vehicle.

(c) By air: any helicopter with a utility designation or greater capability.

(6) Minimal Mission Capability and Setup Timing. Three air traffic controllers can set up the AN/TSQ-97 and provide VFR ATS utilizing UHF/VHF/FM secure communications, provide wind direction, wind speed, and density altitude. The team of 3 can install the AN/TSQ-97 to an operational status within 20 minutes and camouflage it in an additional 10 minutes.

b. Tactical Terminal Control System-AN/TSQ-198.

(1) Description. The AN/TSQ-198 is a new mobile ATC facility, which when fully fielded will replace the AN/TSQ-97. The

AN/TSQ-198 will provide VFR control of air traffic at LZs, drop zones (DZs), pick up zones (PZs), and temporary helicopter operating areas. It can also be used at any LZ where VFR control is required. The AN/TSQ-198 communications system can also be converted to a portable battery-operated manpack (jump) configuration. Major communications components of the AN/TSQ-198 include VHF/UHF AM radio sets and 1 FM radio (single channel ground and airborne radio system [SINCGARS]), 1 HF radio. When the AN/TSQ-198 is used at an airfield, it is only utilized temporarily until larger and more capable facilities are installed. Three air traffic controllers are required for the AN/TSQ-198.

(2) Operations. The AN/TSQ-198 can be operated on a 24-hour-a-day basis. It can move 4 times in a 24-hour period with a total distance of 80 km during the 4 moves with an estimated travel time of 2 hours each move. The AN/TSQ-198 is capable of operations, transportation, and storage in hot, basic, cold, and severe cold climates; it has secure voice communication interface and commonality with other Services. Individuals in mission oriented protective posture (MOPP) IV attire can operate it and the system has been hardened to the effects of NBC contamination and decontamination agents. It is compatible with standard NVDs and has been hardened to the effects of high-altitude electromagnetic pulse.

(3) Interface. The AN/TSQ-198 can interface with other deployed communications facilities via field phones or radios utilizing:

(a) VHF/HF radios with jam resistant capability.

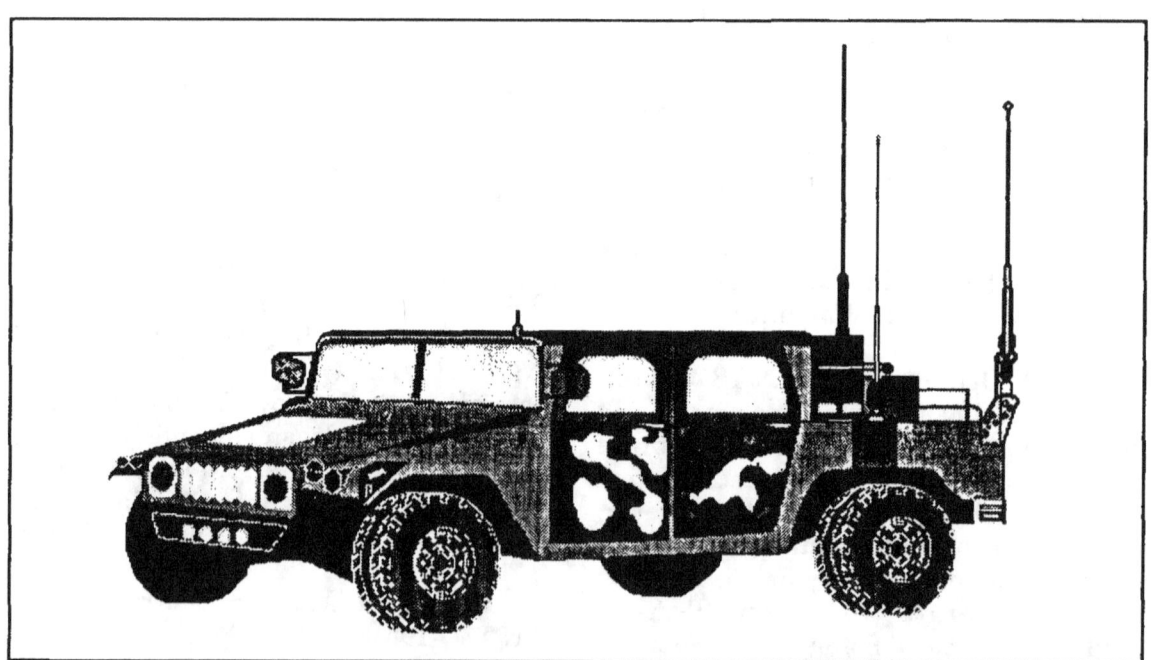

Picture E-1. AN/TSQ-198

(b) UHF, VHF, and HF radios with communications security (COMSEC) capability.

(c) Automatic link establishment for HF.

(d) Data transfer over HF, UHF, and VHF radios.

The AN/TSQ-198 supports standardization and interoperability with other US military radio systems, allied and North Atlantic Treaty Organization (NATO) forces, and with host nation ATS systems. The AN/TSQ-198 is interoperable with the US Air Forces "Pacer Speak" series of radio systems.

(4) Transportation Requirements.

(a) By road: HMMWV, M-998.

(b) By air: sling load, single helicopter capable; C-130 single aircraft minimum requirement.

Note: The AN/TSQ-198 communications system can also be converted to a portable battery-operated manpack (jump) configuration.

(5) Minimal Mission Capability and Setup Timing. Three air traffic controllers set up the AN/TSQ-198 and provide air traffic services utilizing UHF/VHF/FM/HF secure communications. This service includes arrival/departure information, weather, wind direction and speed information, and sequencing instructions. The team of 3 installs the AN/TSQ-198 to an operational status within an estimated 15-30 minutes, including camouflage.

c. Aircraft Control Central-AN/TSQ-70A

(1) Description. Aircraft Control Central AN/TSQ-70A is an air and ground transportable unit that provides facilities for ATC within and about an airfield. The AN/TSQ-70A facilitates visual sighting and communication with aircraft to provide in-flight and on-ground assistance and control. It may be operated from controls inside the shelter or by portable consoles remotely located within 100 feet (ft) radius of the shelter. The AN/TSQ-70A is used at an airfield to provide air traffic regulation, aircraft separation, in-flight assistance, landing and takeoff control, and ground control. Its major components include 3 UHF radios, 3 VHF radios, 2 FM radios, and 1 HF radio. Six air traffic controllers are required for the AN/TSQ-70A.

(2) Interface. The AN/TSQ-70A can interface with other facilities via landline or VHF/UHF/FM/HF radios. *Note: The TSQ-70A uses analog equipment for communications and requires special consideration when interfacing with digital equipment.*

(3) Transportation Requirements.

(a) By ground: M-35 (deuce and a half); sling loaded minus vehicle.

(b) By air: mounted configuration-C-141 or larger; dismounted configuration-C-130 or larger.

(4) Minimal Mission Capability and Setup Timing. After arrival at the required location, the system set up (positions, unpack, and assemble) time is within 1 hour. Required tasks include mounting radio antennas, connecting to the required power source, and performing communications checks.

d. ATC Central-AN/TSW-7A.

(1) Description. The AN/TSW-7A is operated by active duty personnel and provides ground-to-aircraft radio communications and surface communications in a tactical field environment. It is a transportable facility that can be employed at airstrips for airborne and ground control of aircraft. This facility may be installed to

replace permanent control towers in emergency conditions. The ATC central provides the same functions as a stationary ATC tower. It contains all the equipment needed to control aircraft under VFR conditions.

(2) Operation. The ATC central provides ground-to-aircraft, aircraft-to-ground, airborne-to-airborne, and surface communications within a designated airport tactical area or airfield. It also provides 2-way radio communications to aircraft within radio line-of-sight (LOS), weather reporting pilot-to-forecaster service, and flight data. Military operations message relaying is an additional feature. Major components of the AN/TSW-7A include 3 UHF radios, 3 VHF radios, 3 VHF FM/AM radios, and 1 HF radio. Three air traffic controllers are required for the AN/TSW-7A. Four ATC specialists are required for installation of the facility.

(3) Interface. The AN/TSW-7A can interface with other ATC facilities or operations centers via landline (WD-1 or private branch exchange [PBX]), FM, VHF, UHF, and HF radio frequencies. A dual filtered light gun is provided for nonverbal signaling.

(4) Transportation Requirements.

(a) By air: 1 each C-17 (on pallets), C-5 (heavy lift type).

(b) By road: 2 M-35, 2 ½-ton motor vehicles, loaded with baggage and towing MJQ-18 generators.

(5) Minimal Mission Capability and Setup Timing. The AN/TSW-7A is capable of 2 continuous hours of limited operation on battery power. Full service operations on generated power are possible within the limits of equipment maintenance or interoperability. The team can properly position, unpack, and assemble the AN/TSW-7A within 20 minutes (Emergency Mode), 30 minutes (Limited Duration Mode), or 60 minutes (Extended Duration Mode).

e. Landing Control Central-AN/TSQ-71B.

(1) Description. The GCA radar is a precision radar set providing courseline and glidepath tracking of aircraft to within 20 ft (altitude) and 1.3-degree runway alignment of a predetermined landing point (touchdown). Aircraft position as determined by the GCA radar is relayed to the aircraft pilot using the radio communications facilities provided with the AN/TSQ-71B. An airport surveillance radar (ASR) capability may be provided when the maximum radar range is 40 NM. Normally, the search mode is used to vector aircraft into the approach sector. The operating modes, selected by the MODE switch, are—Search Mode, Precision Approach (NORMAL) Mode, Height Finder Mode, Simultaneous Mode (this mode allows tracking targets outside the approach sector while providing GCA [precision] for landing aircraft), and identification, friend, or foe (IFF) interrogation mode. Major components of the AN/TSQ-71B include the shelter, the AS-1905/TPX-44 IFF interrogator antenna, the AN/MJQ-15 power generation set, and the AN/TPN-18 radar set (GCA). Radio communications include 3 UHF radios, 3 VHF radios, and 2 FM radios. Seven air traffic controllers are required for the AN/TSQ-71B.

(2) Interface. AN/TSQ-71B can interface with other facilities via landline or VHF/UHF/FM/HF radios. Normally, the only facility the AN/TSQ-71B will be required to interface with is the tower facility on the same airfield/landing area. *Note: The TSQ-71B uses analog equipment for communications and requires special consideration when interfacing with digital equipment.*

(3) Transportation Requirements.

(a) By road: 2 1/2-ton M-35; sling loaded minus vehicle.

(b) By air: mounted configuration-C-141 or larger; dismounted configuration C-130 or larger.

Note: This system is not rail transportable.

(4) Minimal Mission Capability and Setup Timing. After arrival at the designated location, the GCA team and 7 air traffic controllers can install the AN/TSQ-71B to an operational status and camouflage it within 7 hours.

f. Flight Coordination Center (FCC)-AN/TSC-61B.

(1) Description. The AN/TSC-61B is a transportable unit that provides facilities for air traffic coordination, air defense identification warning, and inflight assistance within an assigned zone of responsibility on a continuous basis. Altitude, time, and distance flight plan data for airborne aircraft can also be coordinated in the FCC (now called an airspace information center [AIC]).

(2) Operation. The AIC is the main ATC facility for the en route structure. It provides facilities to establish air-to-ground radio communications with FM equipment (tactical FM) in the VHF range and with AM equipment (pilot command control) in the UHF, VHF, and HF ranges. There are also facilities for telephone and ground-to-ground radio communications with associated airfields and ground installations, as well as adjacent ATC facilities. Eight air traffic controllers are required for the AN/TSC-61B. The AN/TSC-61B provides the following radio/landline communications capabilities; 3 UHF radios, 3 VHF radios, 3 FM radios, 1 HF radio, and capability for 15 landlines.

(3) Interface. The AN/TSC-61B can interface with other facilities via landline or VHF/UHF/FM/HF radios. The TSC-61B uses analog equipment for communications and requires special consideration when interfacing with digital equipment.

(4) Transportation Requirements.

(a) By road: M-35 or M-211.

(b) By air: sling loaded by utility helicopter when air transported minus the vehicle; in mounted configuration-C-141 or larger; in dismounted configuration-C130 or larger.

(5) Minimal Mission Capability and Setup Timing. After arrival at its tactical location, the AN/TSC-61B can be installed and operational with camouflage within 1 hour. Add 45 minutes for installation of Mast AB-577/GRC (telescoping antenna mast used to raise an array of 2 antennas to a height of approximately 50 ft). Allow an additional 15 minutes for installation of the Extension Kit, Mast MK-806/GRC.

g. Beacon Set, Radio-AN/TRN-30(V) 1/(V)2.

(1) Description. The radio beacon set transmits a homing signal that is used in airborne direction finding (ADF) Sets AN/ARN-59 and AN/ARN-83 installed in helicopters and fixed-wing aircraft. The radio beacon set provides an AM radio frequency (RF) signal on any one of 964 channels in the frequency ranges from 200 to 535.5 kHz and 1605 to 1750.5 kHz in tunable increments of 5 kHz. The RF output is modulated by a 1020 Hz tone, which is automatically keyed to form Morse Code characters in 4-letter groups, as selected by the operator, or manually keyed as desired. The transmission ranges of the radio beacon set are—

(a) AN/TRN-30 (V) 1.

•28 KM (16 NM) with 16 ft antenna.

•46 KM (26 NM) with 30 ft antenna.

(b) AN/TRN-30 (V) 2.

•93 KM (60 NM), tactical mode.

•186 KM (100 NM), semi-fixed mode.

(2) Configurations. The radio beacon set is used to provide a nonprecision approach at a tactical/semi-fixed airfield/landing area in 2 configurations:

(a) Pathfinder mode-AN/TRN-30(V)1.

(b) Tactical and semi-fixed mode-AN/TRN-30 (V) 2.

(3) Personnel. No air traffic controllers are required for this equipment. It is a support NAVAIDS piece of equipment included for use with other ATC facilities.

(4) Interface. N/A.

(5) Transportation Requirements (AN/TRN-30 [V] 1 and [V] 2). Both systems are air or ground transportable. Normally these pieces of equipment are ground transportable by the vehicle/facility using this equipment.

(6) Minimal Mission Capability and Setup Timing. Once the ATC team responsible for siting the radio beacon set has deployed and been provided with a beacon frequency and code they will—

(a) Install to an operational status, the AN/TRN-30 (V) 1 (15 ft antenna) within 20 minutes or (30 ft antenna) within 30 minutes of arrival at desired location (Pathfinder Mode).

(b) Install to an operational status, the AN/TRN-30 (V) 2 (tactical and semi-fixed mode) within 90 minutes of arrival at desired location (Tactical and Semi-fixed Mode).

Table E-1 lists Army ATS equipment, its associated support equipment and the airlift requirements for normal and rapid deployment.

h. Acquisition Programs. Future ATC/ATS Systems which are currently funded.

(1) Tower System (Future)-Mobile Tower System (MOTS).

The MOTS replaces the AN/TSQ-70A and the AN/TSW-7A, Aircraft Control Central. The MOTS is a mobile ATC tower. The MOTS can be deployed mounted on a HMMWV or be air lifted by C-130 aircraft or UH-60 or larger helicopter to the aircraft landing area and rapidly begin operation. The MOTS will provide terminal ATC services for selected high traffic landing areas in the EAC, corps, and division areas. The ATC services will include the necessary coordination permitting IMC recovery and landing with Army precision radar. The MOTS will have digital air/ground communication and digital linkage (mobile subscriber equipment [MSE], Have Quick, SINCGARS, etc.) into A2C2, ATSs, and local command nets. The MOTS will have space for 2 ATC operators and 1 supervisor.

(2) Radar System (Future)-Air Traffic Navigation, Integration, and Coordination System (ATNAVICS).

The ATNAVICS replaces the AN/TSQ-71B, Landing Control Central. The ATNAVICS is a vehicle-mounted, survivable radar system that will provide continuous, near all-weather, landing precision assistance and departure recovery capability at Army tactical airfields and landing areas. Additionally, the ATNAVICS will provide area surveillance and aircraft identification

Table E-1. Army ATS and Support Equipment

ARMY ATS and SUPPORT EQUIPMENT	AIRCRAFT TYPE AMOUNT			
	C-130	C-141	C-17	C-5
TACT		1		1
AN/TSQ-198 Consisting of:				
1 ea M-988 (HMMWV)				
1 ea M-101A2 (Trailer)				
AIC				
Normal Deployment:	3	2	2	1
1 ea M-923A2 (5 Ton Truck)				
1 ea AN/TSC-61B (Comm Van)				
1 ea MJQ-37 (Pwr Gen Trl)				
1 ea M-35A2 (2.5 Ton Truck)				
1 ea M-998 (HMMWV)				
Rapid Deployment:	2	1	2	1
1 ea MJQ-37 (Pwr Gen Trl)				
1 ea AN/TSC-61B (Comm Van)				
1 ea M-998 (HMMWV)				
1 ea M-35A2 (2.5 Ton Truck)				
Tactical Tower Section				
Normal Deployment:	3	2	2	1
1 ea AN/TSW-7A (Cntrl Twr)				
1 ea ECU (for TSW-7A)				
2 ea M35A2 (2.5 Ton Truck)				
2 ea PU-802A (Generators)				
1 ea M-998 (HMMWV)				
1 ea M-101A2 (Trailer)				
Rapid Deployment:	2	1	1	1
1 ea An/TSW-7A (Cntrl Twr)				
2 ea M-35A2 (2.5 Ton Truck)				
2 ea PU-802A (Generators)				
GCA				
Normal Deployment:	4	3	3	1
1 ea AN/TSQ-71 (Radar Shelter)				
1 ea AN/TPN-18A (Rcvr/Trnsmtr)				
1 ea AN/TSC-147 (Comnav Work Van)				
3 ea M-35A2 (2.5 Ton Truck)				
1 ea M-1037 (HMMWV)				
2 ea M-998 (HMMWV)				
2 ea MJQ-39 (Generators)				
1 ea PU-814 (Generator)				
Rapid Deployment:	2	1	1	1
1 ea AN-TSQ-71B (Van)				
1ea AN/TPN-18 (Rcvr/Trnsmtr)				
1 ea M-1037 (HMMWV)				
1 ea M-35A2C (2.5 Ton Truck)				

capability for a minimum of a 25 NM radius of all sites where employed. The ATNAVICS is designed for employment at division, corps, and echelon above corps. The system consists of 3 integrated radars: ASR, precision approach radar (PAR), and secondary surveillance radar. The fixed base PAR is being combined with ATNAVICS for commonality and standardization within the acquisition process.

Picture E-2. Mobile Tower System (MOTS)

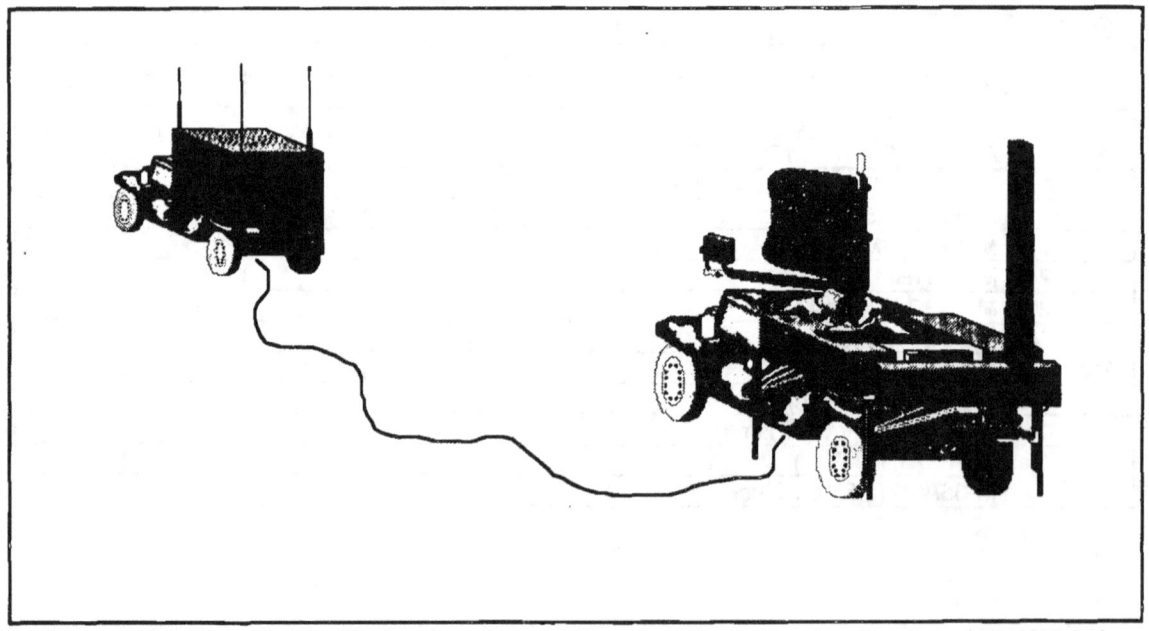

Picture E-3. Air Traffic Navigation, Integration, and Coordination System (ATNAVICS)

(3) A2C2 System (Future)-Tactical Airspace Integration System (TAIS).

The TAIS replaces the AN/TSC-61B Flight Operations Center/Flight Coordination Center (FOC/FCC), and additionally assumes the Army A2C2 mission. The TAIS will be a mobile communications and digitized battlefield automated system for airspace management. FM 100-13, *Battlefield Coordination Detachment (BCD)*, states the TAIS is planned for employment in any theater of operations and will be the Army system to meet both A2C2 and ATS requirements. A2C2 is a combined arms requirement, not just an aviation requirement. The TAIS, as a piece of equipment in the A2C2 element, will be directly responsive to the command level G-3 organization (usually the G-3 Air). The TAIS will collocate with the command level A2C2 element at the main tactical operations center (EAC, corps tactical operations center [CTOC], division tactical operations center [DTOC]), as appropriate. The TAIS will provide the digitized battlefield with automated A2C2 planning, enhanced A2C2 execution, and improved theater and intra- and inter-corps/division ATS support in war, and military operations other than war (MOOTW).

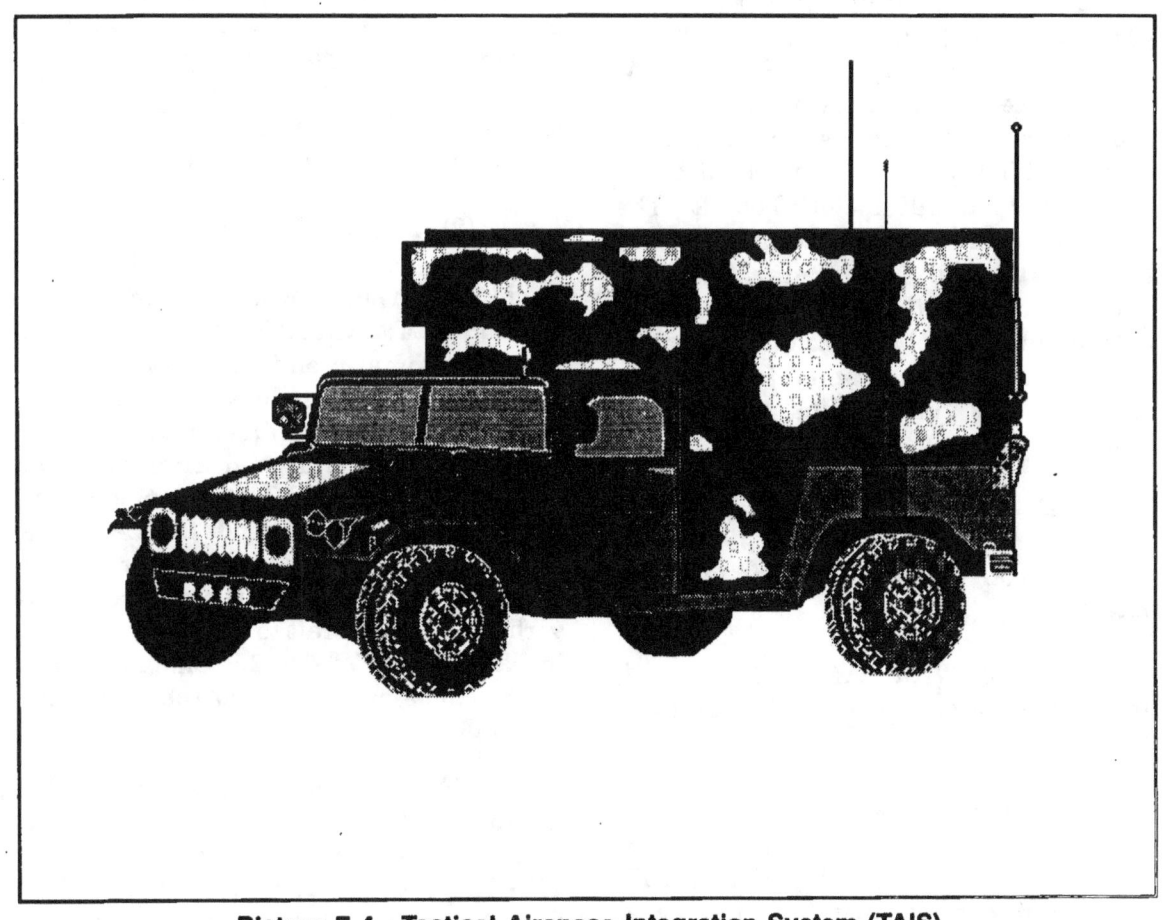

Picture E-4. Tactical Airspace Integration System (TAIS)

3. Marine ATC Equipment

a. Air Traffic Control Section (ATCS)-AN/TPS-73.

(1) Description. The AN/TPS-73 is a 2-dimensional, transportable tactical airport surveillance radar system operating in the E-band (2705-2895 MHz). Designed for a tactical environment with ECM features including blanking sectors and polarization diversity, the AN/TPS-73 is manned and controlled from the AN/TSQ-131, using the AN/TPS-73 control panel. The AN/TPN-73 is enclosed in an International Organization for Standardization (ISO) shelter for independent transport. The antenna drive tilts to permit ground level assembly/disassembly of the 10-piece antenna. The antenna, 16 inch air conditioning ducts, and shelter skids are packed within the shelter. Unmanned during operations, the AN/TPS-73 can be physically located within cable radius (500 ft) of the AN/TSQ-131. The AN/TPN-73 is a nonlinear radar capable of a 60 NM surveillance range for its primary radar, 120 NM search range for its secondary radar (IFF), and is capable of detecting airborne targets up to an altitude of 60,000 ft. The ATCS is capable of interrogating IFF modes I, II, IIIC, and IV. Radar and IFF information from the ATCS are processed within the control and communications subsystem (CCS) and can be forwarded to other agencies via data link and or voice communications.

(2) Interface.

(a) Radio, phone, and intercom access.

(b) With AN/TSQ-131 via orderwire control unit (OCU) or field phone.

(3) Transportation.

(a) By air: C-130, C-141, C-17, C-5, CH-53 can transport as an external load using 40,000 pound slings.

(b) By ground: tractor trailer, logistic vehicle system (LVS).

(4) Setup. The system can be packed-out or set up in 4 hours by 4 Marines.

b. All-Weather Landing Subsystem (ALS)-AN/TPN-22.

(1) Description. The AN/TPN-22 is an I-band (9000-9200 MHz), 3-dimensional, track while search, air transportable, phased array radar that provides the data input to the TSQ-131 for display, enabling controllers to monitor and control aircraft within the landing area airspace. The AN/TPN-22's pencil beam radar has 46-degree azimuth coverage, a 10 NM range, and an 8-degree (minus 1 to plus 7 degrees) angular coverage in elevation. The AN/TPN 22 provides Mode I/IA, Mode II, and Mode III approach services via tactical digital information link (TADIL) C for all-weather landings. The AN/TPN 22 is capable of automatic tracking for up to 6 aircraft simultaneously. The AN/TPN-22 operates in concert with the AN/TSQ-131.

(2) Modes. Mode I is automatic and functions as the landing control and guidance sensor, providing detection and position data to the AN/TSQ-131. Mode II is semiautomatic and provides position, glideslope, and course lines to the TSQ-131 that sends the information to the instruments of equipped aircraft (final controller in AN/TSQ-131 can monitor approach[s]). Mode III sends GCA azimuth/elevation data to the controller in the AN/TSQ-131, allowing the controller to verbally guide aircraft to the runway. Upon initial setup, AN/TPN-22 is unmanned and its functions are monitored remotely from AN/TSQ-131.

(3) Antenna Placement. The number and layout of runways must be considered in antenna placement. The AN/TPN-22 can maintain data on 4 transmitter distributor (TD) points but can provide service to only one runway at a time.

(4) Interface. The AN/TPN-22 provides for transmission of radar, video, antenna, and mode/status information from the AN/TPN-22 to the AN/TSQ-131. Remote control and status panel interface is only operative when the AN/TPN-22 is in auto mode and is required to be fully operable for Mode I and II operations. Voice communication is available between the AN/TPN-22 and the AN/TSQ-131, but the AN/TPN-22 cannot access crypto gear, thus it cannot receive covered communications from the AN/TSQ-131.

(5) Transportation Requirements.

(a) By air: C-130, C-141, C-5, CH-53 can transport as an external load using 40,000 pound slings.

(b) By ground: tractor trailer, LVS.

(6) Setup. Three Marines can site-survey and set up the system for 1 runway within 3 hours.

c. CCS-AN/TSQ-131.

(1) Description. The AN/TSQ-131 is the heart of the Marine air traffic control and landing system (MATCALS). It is an air transportable facility containing all equipment, excluding sensors, to meet display and communications requirements for providing full IFR ATC services to expeditionary airfields. It functions as a collection point for radar data produced by the ATCS and the ALS. The CCS consists of 2 ISO shelters, which allow its employment in either a single or dual shelter configuration. Each shelter provides 4 processor display system (PDS) consoles, which serve as operational workstations for crewmembers. Each PDS has its own communications capability. In addition to intercommunications and switchboard circuits, the CCS provide access to 1 HF, 3 VHF amplitude modulation (AM), 1 VHF FM, and 8 UHF radios. One UHF radio is reserved for

TADIL-C. In addition to accessing single channel radios, the CCS provides access to 10 external telephone lines. The CCS has the capability to automatically exchange certain elements of command, tactical intelligence, and situation data with other MATCDs, TAOCs, and the TACC via TADIL-B. The AN/TSQ-131 has a 20-channel tape recorder and has secure voice capability using KY-75 and KY-58. The CCS is a software driven system.

(2) Interface.

(a) Provides for digital interface (not video) of control and data messages between various peripherals.

(b) Remote control units located within the AN/TSQ-131 to provide status and remote control of the AN/TPN-22, AN/TPS-73 and AN/TRN-44.

(c) With TSQ-120A by OCU radios and field phones.

(d) External agencies (weather, VFR, air operations) by field phones and ground to ground radio nets.

(e) Crash alarm wired from tower.

(3) Transportation Requirements.

(a) By air: C-130, C-141, C-17, C-5, CH-53 can transport as an external load.

(b) By ground: tractor trailer, LVS.

(4) Setup.

(a) 6 Marines can set up 1 AN/TSQ-131 in 2 hours.

(b) 6 Marines can set up 2 AN/TSQ-131s in 5 hours.

(c) Two AN-TSQ-131s with 1 AN/TPS-73 and 1 AN/TPN-22 can be set up in 10 hours by 12 Marines.

d. Air Traffic Control Central (ATC Tower)-AN/TSQ-120A/B.

(1) Description. The AN/TSQ-120 is a transportable ATC tower facility, which provides operators with 360-degree visual observance of aircraft, both on the ground and in the air, operating within a designated control zone and visual control over ground vehicles operating in the vicinity of the runway. The ATC tower can be erected to heights of 8, 16, or 24 ft. The ATC tower provides the operator positions from where aircraft and airfield control is effected through the use of radio communications and visual aids. The ATC tower provides operators with access to 1 HF, 3 VHF/AM, 1 VHF/FM, and 5 UHF single channel radios and up to 10 telephone lines. The AN/TSQ-120B model is capable of encrypted communications, has a second crash net radio, and is equipped with an ISO shelter. All audio communications are recorded.

(2) Interface. The AN/TSQ-120A/B must deploy with at least 1 AN/TQS-131 and AN/TPS-73 during IFR/IMC conditions. Aircraft operations may coordinate with AN/TSQ-131 by field phone. Crash, fire, and rescue coordination are done with crash radio or landline. Communication assets include radios and phone lines. *Note: The radios come from the AN/TSQ-131, thus reducing the AN/TSQ-131's capability.*

(3) Transportation Requirements.

(a) By air: C-130, C-141, C-17, C-5.

(b) By ground: tractor trailer, LVS, 5 ton.

(4) Setup. 4 Marines can erect the system to a height of 24 ft within 5 hours.

e. Control Central-AN/TRC-195.

(1) Description. The AN/TRC-195 provides a limited tower capability for remote site operations. Typically employed in the rear section of a HMMWV, the AN/TRC-195 provides up to 2 controllers with communications access to 4 20 Hz telephone lines and 1 HF/VHF FM, 1 VHF AM, and 2 UHF single channel radios.

(2) Interface.

(a) Landlines with AN/TSQ-131 and or AN/TSQ-120 when used as a tower backup.

(b) With AN/TPN-30.

(c) Communication via radios. *Note: The radios come from the AN/TSQ-131, thus reducing the AN/TSQ-131's capability.*

(3) Transportation Requirements.

(a) By air: C-130, C141, C-17, C-5, CH-53, CH-46.

(b) By ground: flatbed, HMMWV or equivalent, railroad cars, short distances forklift.

(4) Setup. 30 minutes by 2 Marines.

f. Tactical Air Navigation (TACAN)-AN/TRN-44.

(1) Description. The AN/TRN-44 set is a transportable, dual-channel navigational aid which operates in the D-band (962-1213 MHz) and provides up to 100 TACAN equipped aircraft with range, bearing and station identification information within an effective radius coverage of 200 miles. It is used for both en route navigation guidance and as an instrument approach aid.

(2) Interface.

(a) Linked by phone land lines with AN/TSQ-120 and/or AN/TSQ-131.

(b) Linked to other units by field phones.

(c) If employed alone, technicians man it; if it is employed with the AN/TSQ-120 or AN/TSQ-131, it is unmanned and remotely monitored.

(3) Transportation Requirements.

(a) By air: C-130, C-141, C-17, C-5.

(b) By ground: tractor trailer, LVS, 5 ton.

(4) Setup. 4 hours by 4 Marines.

g. Marine Remote Area Approach and Landing System (MRAALS)-AN/TPN-30.

(1) Description. The AN/TPN-30 is a 2-person, portable, all-weather instrument landing system. It transmits azimuth, distance, and elevation data in the J-band (15.412-15.680 GHz) and distance measuring equipment (DME)/station identification data in the D-band (962-1213 MHz). It provides 40-degree azimuth and 20-degree elevation guidance out to 10 NM on final approach to aircraft equipped with the ARA-63 airborne radar system. It also provides 360-degree DME and station identification information out to 40 NM. The AN/TPN-30 will be used as independent landing monitors in conjunction with the AN/TPN-22. The AN/TPN-30 will provide the pilot an in-cockpit check of the approach that is independent of the AN/TPN-22 system.

(2) Interface.

(a) Can be monitored from AN/TSQ-120 or can be remotely controlled up to 1000 ft using field wire.

(b) Communication via radio link interface set that uses VHF 30.00-75.95 (with 50 KHz spacing).

(3) Transportation Requirements.

(a) By air: C-130, C-141, C-17, C-5, CH-53, CH-46, UH-1N.

(b) By ground: tractor trailer, LVS 5-ton, HMMWV or equivalent.

(4) Setup. 10-15 minutes by 2 Marines.

h. Maintenance Repair Group-AN/TSM-170.

(1) Description. The AN/TSM-170 group consists of 4 standard ISO shelters, which contain the workbenches, test equipment, cabinets, tools, and other equipment necessary for section maintenance of Fleet Marine Force (FMF) ATC equipment. All shelters allow some degree of flexibility to accommodate changed maintenance demands based on mission and equipment configuration. The AN/TSM-170 group consists of the following shelters:

(a) OA-9141/TSM-170-Auxiliary Equipment Repair Group.

(b) OA-9142/TSM-170-Communications Equipment Repair Group.

(c) OA-9143/TSM-170-Radar Equipment Repair Group.

(d) OA-9144/TSM-170-Electronic Module Repair Group.

(2) Interface. With other FMF ATC equipment is by field phone.

(3) Transportation Requirements.

(a) By air: C-130, C-141, C-17, C-5, CH-53 can transport as an external load.

(b) By ground: tractor trailer, LVS.

(4) Setup. Each AN/TSM-170 is configured for immediate deployment and requires 30 minutes setup time.

Table E-2 lists amphibious ATC equipment.

Table E-2. Amphibious ATC Equipment

HULL UIC	SHIP	CURRENT DISPLAY	LOAD DTS	FUTURE DISPLAY DLVR	CDC SYSTEM	COM SUITE	PLAY BACK	HEADSET JACKBOX	PAR	SPN-41A ILS	NAV SRCE	RADARS/IFF
LHA-1 20550	TARAWA (SAN DIEGO)	NTDS UYA-4	N/A	TPX-42V-13 V-XX ADS 2ND QTR FY 99	NTDS ACDS BLK 1 2-99	LS537 IVN-98	RD390	(10) (8)	SPN-35B	FY01	KCMX	SPN43B, 52, 40, 67 IFF - SAME
LHA-2 20632	SAIPAN (NORFOLK)	TPX-42V12 V002.Y8 OD201	USH-26 USQ69	TPX-42V-13 V-XX ADS 2ND QTR FY 04	ACDS B0/L10	LS537 IVN-01	RD379A SPKR	10 8	SPN-35B	FY01	ACDS KCMX	SPN43C, 48E, 40, 67 IFF - 43, 48 (CIFF)
LHA-3 20633	BELLEAU WOOD (JAPAN)	TPX-42V13 V002.Y9 OD201	USH-26 USQ69	TPX-42V-13 V-XX ADS 2ND QTR FY 04	NTDS ACDS B0/L10 3-98	LS537 IVN-01	RC3212 SPKR	10 8	SPN-35A	FY99	SPN-25 KCMX	SPN43C, 48E,40, 67 IFF - SAME
LHA-4 20725	NASSAU (NORFOLK)	TPX-42V-13 V002.Y8 OD201	USQ69B-D USQ69B-S	TPX-42V-13 V-XX ADS 2ND QTR FY 04	ACDS B0/L10	LS537 IVN-99	RC3212 SPKR	10 8	SPN-35B	FY02	ACDS KCMX	SPN43B, 48E, 40, 67 IFF - 43, 48 (CIFF)
LHA-5 20748	PELELIU (SAN DIEGO)	TPX-42V13 V002.Y9 OD-201	USQ69B-D USQ69B-S	TPX-42V-13 V-XX ADS 2ND QTR FY 04	NTDS ACDS BLK 1 9-98	LS537 IVN-01	RC3212 SPKR	10 8	SPN-35B	FY03	PCNAV KCMX	SPN43C, 48E, 40, 67 IFF - SAME
LHD-1 21590	WASP (NORFOLK)	TPX-42V-12 V001 OD-201	USH-26 USQ69	TPX-42V-12/V002.Y8 OD-201 OCT 97 TPX-42V-13 V-XX ADS 3RD QTR FY 03	ACDS BLK 1	LS664	RD379A SPKR	10 8	SPN-35B	DONE	SDMS KCMX	SPN43C, 49, 48E, 67 IFF - 43, 49
LHD-2 21533	ESSEX (SAN DIEGO)	TPX-42V12 V002.Y8 OD-201	USH-26 USQ69	TPX-42V-13 V-XX ADS 3RD QTR FY 04	ACDS BLK 0/L 9	LS664	RD379A	10 8	SPN-35B	FY01	SDMS KCMX	SPN43C, 49, 48E, 67 IFF - 43, 49
LHD-3 21700	KEARSARGE (NORFOLK)	TPX-42V12 V002.Y8 OD-201	USH-26 USQ69	TPX-42V-13 V-XX ADS 2ND QTR FY 03	ACDS BLK 0/L 10	LS664	RD379A	10 8	SPN-35B	FY98	SDMS KCMX	SPN43C, 49, 48E, 67 IFF - 43, 49
LHD-4 21808	BOXER (SAN DIEGO)	TPX-42V12 V002.Y8 OD-201	USH-26 USQ69	TPX-42V-13 V-XX ADS 4TH QTR FY 04	ACDS BLK 0/L 9	LS664	RD379A	10 8	SPN-35A	FY01	SDMS KCMX	SPN43B, 49, 48E, 67 IFF - 43, 49
LHD-5 21879	BATAAN (NORFOLK)	TPX-42V13 V002.Y8 OD-201	USQ69B-S USQ69B-D	TPX-42V-13 V-XX ADS 2ND QTR FY 04	ACDS BLK 0/L 10	PICT	RC3212 SPKR	10	SPN-35B	DONE	SDMS KCMX	SPN43C, 49, 48E, 67 IFF - 43,49
LHD-6 22202	BON HOMME RICHARD (SAN DIEGO)	TPX-42V13 V002.Y8 OD-201	USH-26 USQ69B-S	TPX-42V-13 V-XX ADS 2ND QTR FY 04	ACDS BLK 0/L 10	PICT	RC3212	(10)	SPN-35B	DONE	SDMS KCMX	SPN43C, 49, 48E, 67 IFF - 43, 49
LHD-7	IWO JIMA (NORFOLK)		USH-26 USQ69B-S	TPX-42V-13 V-XX ADS 2ND QTR FY 00	ACDS BLK 0/L 10	PICT	WORD SAFE RD390	(10)	SPN-35B	FY00	SDMS KCMX	SPN43C, 49, 48E, 67 IFF - 43, 49
MCS-12	INCHON (INGALSIDE)	SPA-25G RPTR	N/A	N/A	LINK 14	TA970	RD390	5 4	SPN-35B	N/A	GYRO	SPN43B

Amphibious ATC Equipment - equipment and displays are being updated on several ships, which are depicted.

4. Air Force ATC Equipment.

a. Special Tactics Squadrons (STS). In addition to the AN/MRC-144, AN/TRN-41 TACAN, AN/TRN-45 Mobile Microwave Landing System (MMLS) and airfield marking equipment, the STS possess the following equipment:

(1) VHF/UHF Manpack Radios

(a) AN/PRC-113 Transceiver. This equipment operates in secure and non-secure voice mode. It can be used for Have Quick/whisper mode operation(s).

(b) PRC-117D(C) Transceiver. This equipment operates in simplex/half duplex mode. It has a frequency hopping mode and satellite communications (SATCOM) mode of operation. The equipment also has a built in COMSEC module.

(c) LST-5C Lightweight Satellite Transceiver. This equipment operates in FM and AM scan and beacon modes. It has a self-contained 1200/2400 baud modem.

(d) HST-4A Satellite Transceiver. This equipment operates in AM scan and beacon modes and also has a secure mode of operations in AM/FM. It has a self-contained 1200/2400 baud modem.

(2) HF Manpack Radios.

(a) AN/PRC-132 HF Transceiver. This equipment operates in single sideband (SSB) and half duplex mode. It has 100 programmable transmit (TX) and receive (RX) channels.

(b) AN/PRC-138 Manpack Tactical HF Radio. This equipment operates side band (SB)/lower side band (LSB)/upper side band (USB). It also operates FSK/frequency hopping and hopping half duplex mode.

(3) Handheld Radios.

(a) AN/PRC-112 Survival Radio. This equipment provides 121.5 and 243 MHz beacon and allows interrogation by personal locator system (PLS) avionics system. The equipment has 2 programmable channels in UHF range.

(b) AN/PRC-126/8 VHF Radio Set. This equipment has 10 programmable channels. It watertight up to 10 ft. It is secure capable with KYV-2A. It also operates in FM simplex or half-duplex modes.

(c) AN/PRC-139 VHF/UHF FM Transceiver. This equipment has 14 programmable channels. It provides Vinson/Fascinator interoperability.

(d) Saber II and Saber III Portable Radios. These radios have 12 programmable channels with an optional secure capability with Fascinator. The equipment is field programmable.

(4) Communications Systems.

AN/MRC-144 Mobile Communications System. This system can operate in HF SSB, VHF AM/FM, and UHF AM. The system contains an additional mount for AN/PSN-11 global positioning system (GPS) plugger equipment.

(5) Beacons and Transponders.

(a) PRD-7880 Selectable Strike Beacon. This equipment is used with the ASD-5 Black Crow System on the AC-130H Gunship. It provides target identification, range, azimuth, and beacon identification/idea. It is used in a "no communications" environment.

(b) SST-124 Transponder. This equipment is used to mark and drop LZs for MC-130E Combat Talon One. It receives 1 frequency while transmitting up to 16 different code combinations on another frequency.

(c) SST-181 Transponder. This equipment is used as a radar reference point in marking assault landing and DZs. The equipment marks friendly positions during AC-130H/U Gunship call-for-fire missions.

(d) AN/PPN-19 Multiband Transponder. This equipment is used as a radar reference point in offset beacon bombing and naval gunfire. It is also used to identify friendly positions. It is compatible with most radar equipped aircraft including AC-130H/U and MC-130 E/H.

(6) Laser Equipment.

(a) GCP-1 Ground Commander's Pointer. This equipment contains a safety switch to prevent accidental laser emissions. It also has a laser output lens to adjust the beam's intensity.

(b) GCP-1A Ground Commanders Pointer. This equipment has the remote switch function. The safety cover must be in the armed position before the equipment can be activated with the on/off switch

b. General Purpose USAF ATC Equipment.

(1) Landing Control Central-AN/TPN-19.

(a) Description. The active duty operated and maintained AN/TPN-19 Landing Control Central (Radar Set) can be configured as a complete radar approach control (RAPCON) with radar final control (RFC), RAPCON with ASR only, or a GCA only facility. The radar unit is used by air traffic controllers to locate and identify arriving and departing aircraft and provide final approach guidance. These services can be provided in all types of weather.

(b) Capabilities. The radar unit is capable of identifying aircraft using secondary radar within a 200 NM radius, SFC-60,000 ft, and primary radar coverage to 60 NM, SFC-40,000 ft. The PAR portion provides both azimuth and elevation

information from 20 NM to touchdown. The unit has 6 display indicators that are capable of providing both ASR and PAR displays in the operations shelter.

With all these indicators and communications equipment installed, the unit is capable of taking over ATC operations at busy airports. Since the PAR antenna may be rotated and locked into numerous positions, the unit is capable of providing approaches to 4 runways.

(c) Personnel. ATC personnel required include 2 air traffic controllers from a combat communications group (CCG) and 18 air traffic controllers (unit type code [UTC]-tasked from fixed base assets).

(d) Interface. The AN/TPN-19 can interface with other facilities via landline or UHF/VHF radio. These facilities include other ATC facilities and wing operations centers. *Note: The TPN-19 uses analog equipment for communications, and requires special consideration when interfacing with digital equipment.*

(e) Transportation Requirements. Transportation Requirements for the AN/TPN-19 consist of the following:

• By air: 7 C-130s or 3 C-141s or 1 C-5 (36 pallet positions without self-propelled vehicles).

• By road:

•• M-923 loaded with mobility readiness spares package (MRSP) towing PAR shelter.

•• M-923 loaded with MRSP towing ASR shelter.

•• M-923 loaded with support towing Ops A shelter

•• M-923 loaded with support towing Ops B shelter.

••M-35 loaded with power support towing ASR/OPS pallet.

••M-35 towing S530A shelter.

••M-35 loaded with MRSP, towing S530B shelter or 280 shelter.

••M-35 loaded with life support, towing the PAR pallet.

••M-35 loaded with fuel drums, towing mobile electric power (MEP) 005.

••M-35 loaded with fuel drums, towing MEP 005.

••M-35 loaded with baggage, towing MEP 005.

••M-35 loaded with support towing MEP 005.

••M-35 loaded with support towing MEP 006.

••M-35 loaded with support towing MEP 006.

(f) Minimal Mission Capability and Setup Timing. Ten maintenance personnel should be able to install the AN/TPN-19 with 1 operational PAR scope, 2 operational ASR scopes, secondary radar, 4 UHF, and 2 VHF radios within 26 hours. Prior to being declared mission capable the AN/TPN-19 must receive a flight inspection. *Note: Under combat limited situations with no augmentees assigned, the standard time is 36 hours.*

(2) Landing Control Central-AN/ MPN-14K.

(a) Description. The Air National Guard (ANG) operated and maintained AN/MPN-14K Landing Control Central (Instrument Landing Aid) can be configured as a complete RAPCON with RFC, RAPCON with ASR only, or a GCA only facility. The system can deploy autonomously configured as a GCA only facility providing limited final approach guidance. The radar unit is used by air traffic controllers to locate and identify arriving and departing aircraft and provide final approach guidance. These services can be provided in all types of weather.

(b) Capabilities. The radar unit is capable of providing 60 NM primary radar coverage, SFC–40,000 ft and 200 NM secondary, SFC–60,000 ft IFF/Selective Identification Feature IFF/SIF sweep coverage. The PAR portion provides both azimuth and elevation information from 20 NM to touchdown. The unit has 3 ASR indicators and 1 PAR indicator in the operations shelter. The unit is capable of ATC operations at busy airports with single runway operations. The radar unit is capable of providing dual runway operations with the use of a portable turntable.

(c) Personnel. ATC personnel required are 1 air traffic control officer, 16 air traffic controllers, and 1 TERPS specialist.

(d) Interface. The AN/MPN-14K is capable of interface with the AN/TSW-7 mobile control tower and other facilities via landline, radio (UHF/VHF), and microwave link. *Note: Under combat limited situations with no augmentees assigned, the standard time is 36 hours.* The system uses analog equipment for communications and requires special consideration when interfacing with digital equipment.

(e) Transportation Requirements. Transportation requirements for the AN/MPN-14K consist of the following:

•By air: 3 C-130s or 1 C-5

•By road:

••M-923 loaded with MSRP towing ops shelter.

••M-923 loaded with support towing maintenance shelter.

••M-35 loaded with fuel drums, towing MEP 806B generator.

••M-35 loaded with support towing MEP 806B generator.

••M-35 loaded with support cables.

(f) Minimal Mission Capability and Setup Timing. Eleven maintenance and 16 ATC personnel are required to install the AN/MPN-14K with 1 operational PAR scope, 3 operational ASR scopes, secondary radar, 4 UHF, and 2 VHF radios within 24 hours. Prior to being declared mission capable, the AN/MPN-14K must receive a flight inspection after setup.

(3) ATC Central-AN/TSW-7.

(a) Description. The AN/TSW-7 is a Mobile Control Tower, operated and maintained by both active duty and ANG personnel is used to provide ATC capabilities where no operational control tower exists (bare base operations). The AN/TSW-7 has limited capabilities; however, it provides controllers with the minimum items necessary to do the job.

(b) Communications. The AN/TSW-7 provides air traffic controllers landlines, UHF/VHF radios, crash phone, emergency warning and evacuation alarm signal, barometer, tape recorders, binoculars, NAVAIDS monitor, light guns, and wind measuring equipment.

(c) Personnel. There are 3 controller positions: local control (controls airborne aircraft and runway traffic), ground control (controls all other ground movements, aircraft and vehicles), and flight data (handles administrative coordination).

ATC personnel required include 2 air traffic controllers (from active duty CCG or ANG UTC-tasked) and 8 air traffic controllers (ANG or active duty fixed base UTC-tasked).

(d) Interface. The AN/TSW-7 can interface with other facilities via landline or radio (UHF/VHF). Other facilities include the AN/MPN-14K or AN/TPN-19 as well as on base fixed facilities or off-base radar approach/center facilities. The AN/TSW-7 is also capable of monitoring the AN/TRN-26 mobile TACAN.

(e) Transportation Requirements. Transportation requirements for the AN/TSW-7 consist of the following:

•By air: 2 C-130s or 1 C-141 (11 pallet positions, without self-propelled vehicles).

•By road:

••M-35 loaded with MRSP/field support, AN/TSW-7 on M-720 mobilizers.

••M-35 loaded with MRSP/field support, towing support pallet on M-720 mobilizers.

••M-35 loaded with baggage, towing MEP-005A/M-200 trailer.

••M-35 towing MEP-005A/M-200 trailer.

(f) Minimal Mission Capability and Setup Timing. Seven maintenance personnel should have the mobile tower operational with 3 UHF radios plus a 243.0 UHF guard receiver, 2 VHF radios plus 121.5 VHF guard receiver, and 1 light gun within 16 hours. After the unit is fully operational the number of maintenance personnel required decreases.

(4) Tower Restoral Vehicle (TRV)-AN/MSN-7.

(a) Description. The AN/MSN-7 is currently in the final field testing phases and is programmed to replace the AN/TSW-7 in both the active duty and ANG inventories. The system consists of a vehicle-mounted shelter containing ATC control equipment and space for 3 air traffic controller personnel to perform aircraft launch and recovery operations. Transported to the theater of operations by air, it can be driven to its final operating location, set up quickly, and capable of self-sustained operation in a bare-base environment. If necessary, the system can be quickly torn down and moved to a new operating location. The system's communications capabilities are robust, allowing the AN/MSN-7 to temporarily replace existing ATC tower facilities while they are being repaired or refurbished.

(b) Threats. The AN/MSN-7 mission, to supply ATC service in bare-base locations, may make the system a primary target of surface-to-surface and air-to-surface munitions. Although the AN/MSN-7 may be located in vulnerable areas during an attack against the airfield, the system's high mobility and relatively small size will allow its crew to react quickly and move the system to a sheltered area. A threat also exists from hostile special operations forces. Due to its small size and weight, small arms fire and lightweight explosives easily damage the AN/MSN-7. A secondary threat is present due to the AN/MSN-7's close proximity to other primary targets on the airfield. The system could suffer collateral damage if it is near one of these targets during an airfield attack. Survivability may be aided by camouflage and the fact that emissions from the AN/MSN-7 need be present only during aircraft launch and recovery operations. Electronic warfare and electronic countermeasures will be a partial jamming threat to communications used by the system. The use of Have Quick capable radios will give antijam protection to UHF communications.

(c) Capabilities. During wartime, the AN/MSN-7 is capable of being quickly deployed and operating in a bare base environment. Forward operating locations demand that the system be self-supporting. If hostile airfields are captured, the AN/MSN-7 is capable of rapid redeployment to the captured area in order to exploit these resources and render ATC service to friendly forces.

The system will remain mostly in a nonoperational state (in storage) during peacetime. The storage requirements allow storage almost anywhere space is available. The system can be rapidly readied and transported to locations where ATC service has been lost due to natural disaster. Once there, the system will supply temporary service until repairs are made to fixed tower assets. The system is designed to be set up and operational under all expected environmental conditions.

(d) Personnel. The proposed number of ATC personnel required to operate the AN/MSN-7 include 2 air traffic controllers (from active duty CCG or ANG UTC-tasked) and 8 air traffic controllers (ANG or active duty fixed base UTC-tasked).

(e) Interface. The AN/MSN-7 is interoperable with the host wing C2 structure for fixed base operations. The AN/MSN-7 does not require a wing command and control system workstation. Any communications with Theater Air Control or the Airlift Control System will take place via radio or landline. Frequency allocations for ground-to-air radios are such that operation of the AN/MSN-7 is transparent to aircraft supported by ATC operations conducted from the AN/MSN-7 within the constraints of the system's intended mission. Frequency allocations for the land mobile radios (LMRs) ensure interoperability with other base functions such as communications squadrons and base operations. Since the AN/MSN-7 operates in foreign countries, interface and interoperability considerations with existing and potential allied ATC and C2 systems are imperative.

(f) Transportation Requirements. A single AN/MSN-7 system must be transportable without disassembly by 1 C-130 aircraft. This requirement is limited to the prime mover and support vehicle; it does not include manpower or all the necessary sustainment equipment detailed in the UTC. The AN/MSN-7 can be driven to its operating location using either unimproved roads or, if necessary, by crossing moderately rough open terrain. The ability to travel at a 50 mph cruising speed on paved roads enables the AN/MSN-7 to be driven reasonable distances from its storage location to embarkation point or from its debarkation point to its operating location. This capability conserves airlift sorties.

(g) Minimal Mission Capability and Setup Timing. The AN/MSN-7 is capable of being made fully operational within 1.5 hours nominal, after arrival on site by a maximum of 4 trained personnel. AN/MSN-7 setup time will be no more than 2 hours when these personnel are wearing chemical, biological, and radiological (CBR) or arctic weather gear. The same time and personnel constraints apply to the system when dismantling and packing for storage or redeployment.

(5) TACAN-AN/TRN-26.

(a) Description. The active duty and ANG operated and maintained AN/TRN-26 is designed for use at remote landing strips and forward operating areas. The system provides radio navigation information (azimuth or bearing, identification, and range) to as many as 100 aircraft simultaneously. Due to the UHF carrier, the transmitted information is limited to LOS.

(b) Capabilities. The system has an acquisition range of 35 NM at 1500 ft above unobstructed terrain and a maximum reception range of 100 NM. Associated monitoring equipment provides a continuous check of all significant TACAN

parameters and shuts the TACAN off when a fault occurs. The AN/TRN-26A is not suitable for deployments longer than 30 days, or to areas likely to experience extreme weather conditions, without environmental control provisions.

(c) Interface. The AN/TRN-26 does not require interface with other facilities. However, it normally has a monitor connected to the RAPCON or tower to allow 24-hour monitoring.

(d) Transportation Requirements.

•By air: 1 C-130 or 1 C-141 (AN/TRN-26A 2 pallet positions, AN/TRN-26B 3 pallet positions without self-propelled vehicle).

•By road:

••AN/TRN-26A: M-923 loaded with MRSP and AN/TRN-26A TACAN.

••M-35 loaded with, 2 MEP-003A.

(e) Minimal Mission Capability and Setup Timing. All assigned maintenance personnel should have the TACAN operational within 4 hours. At least 1 integral monitor and 1 receiver/transmitter with 63-channel capability identification, and at least 360-watt output power are required before the TACAN can be declared operational. Prior to being declared mission capable the AN/TRN-26 must receive a flight inspection.

(6) TACAN-AN/TRN-41.

(a) Description. The AN/TRN-41 is a portable, lightweight, air dropable, unmanned TACAN designed to provide bearing, facility identification, and distance information. The ground equipment consists of a transponder with associated antenna system and the aircraft is equipped with an interrogator. The TACAN transmits continuous bearing information to an unlimited number of aircraft and provides slant range distance information to as many as 100 aircraft simultaneously. Due to the UHF carrier, the transmitted information is limited to LOS use only with a range of 75 NM. This TACAN does not possess external azimuth monitoring device as required by AFMAN 11-225; therefore, it is not currently certified for IFR use. A programmed modification to this system will make this system IFR-capable in the future.

(b) Interface. The AN/TRN-41 does not require any other type of equipment to be operational.

(c) Transportation Requirements.

•By air: 1 C-130 or 1 C-141 (1 pallet position, without self-propelled vehicle).

•By road: 1 M-35 with AN/TRN-41 TACAN/generator/generator MRSP/support.

(d) Minimal Mission Capability and Setup Timing. Three meteorological/navigational aid technicians should set up 63 channels with identification and at least 100 watts of power output in 4 hours.

(7) Mobile HF/UHF/VHF Radio System-AN/MRC-144.

(a) Description. The AN/MRC-144 is a mobile HF/VHF/UHF communications facility with an AN/GRC-206 package mounted in an M-998 HMMWV. It provides SSB HF, VHF/FM, VHF/AM, and UHF communications, with a full compliment of portable backup radios. This system can be remotely operated up to 2 km away. All radios have secure voice capability. When used in an ATC capacity, air traffic controllers must be tasked separately. Four air traffic controllers (modified UTC from fixed base assets) are required.

(b) Interface. The AN/MRC-144 can communicate with any radio in the UHF/VHF AM, VHF FM, and HF range. Also, it can communicate with any UHF AM radio that has been modified with Have Quick II.

(c) Transportation Requirements.

•By air: 1 C-130 or One C-141 (5 pallet positions, includes 1 self-propelled vehicle [M-998]).

•By road: M-998 HMMWV and towing M-101 trailer.

(d) Minimal Mission Capability and Setup Timing. One radio technician and 1 radio operator should have HF/SSB, VHF/FM, UHF/AM, and VHF/AM radios available over 90 percent of the tuning range in 45 minutes.

(8) VHF/UHF-AM Radio Set-AN/TRC-176.

(a) Description. The AN/TRC-176 is a portable UHF/VHF radio set operating in the 116.0 to 149.975 or 225.0 to 399.975 MHz frequency bands. It can provide 1 channel of either UHF or VHF voice communications (both UHF and VHF cannot be operated simultaneously) and can be secured with TSEC/KY-57 and operate in the Have Quick mode to prevent enemy jamming. This system, although not a part of DATCALS, acts as an important backup ATC communications capability in the event of degraded operations from the ATC deployable systems.

(b) Capabilities. Air-to-ground radio operations encompass the majority of missions for this system, although it can be used for local command and control and engineering nets. The operational range for local area ground-to-ground communications is less than 35 miles with minimal obstructions between communications points. For air-to-ground the operational range is up to 200 miles LOS.

(c) Interface. The AN/TRC-176 can interface with all VHF/UHF radio systems that operate in the 116-149.95 or 225-400 MHz range and have a 25 kHz or higher separation between channels. Some older UHF systems can only select channels at 50 kHz increments so these systems may not tune to all the frequencies available on the AN/TRC-176.

(d) Transportation Requirements.

•By air: 1 C-130 or 1 C-141 (1 pallet position, without self-propelled vehicles).

•By road: M-35 loaded with MRSP, radios, and antennas.

(e) Minimal Mission Capability and Setup Timing. One ground radio technician should have 8 watts of power over 90 percent of the VHF and UHF tuning ranges within 4 hours.

(9) Mobile Microwave Landing System-AN/TRN-45.

(a) Description. The MMLS provides precision navigation guidance for exact aircraft alignment and descent of aircraft on approach to a selected runway by providing 3-dimensional navigation guidance. It integrates azimuth, elevation angle, and range DME information to provide precise aircraft positioning. The components of an MMLS are similar to an instrument landing system (ILS). There is a glideslope antenna known as an elevation station and a localizer antenna known as an azimuth station.

(b) Capabilities. The MMLS can fulfill a variety of needs in the transition, approach, landing, missed approach, and departure phases of flight. Some additional capabilities associated with MMLS include curved and segmented approaches, selectable glideslope angles, accurate 3-dimensional positioning of the aircraft in space, and the establishment of boundaries to ensure clearance from obstructions in the terminal area. The azimuth coverage extends laterally to allow for proportional coverage or clearance signal to at least plus or minus 400 ft on either side of the runway. In elevation, coverage extends from the horizon (00 degrees) up to an angle of 150 degrees and up to at least 20,000 ft, and in range to a maximum of 15 NM. The elevation station transmits its guidance signals on the same carrier frequency as the azimuth station. The single frequency is time-shared between angle and data function. Coverage extends to a distance of at least 15 NM. MMLS has 200 discrete channels.

The system has low susceptibility to interference from weather conditions and airport ground traffic, but has a high susceptibility to television signals.

(c) Interface. MMLS is normally installed in a configuration quite similar to ILS; however, it is possible, if necessary because of limited space, to install all of the components together. In a standard airfield installation, the MMLS azimuth transmitter is usually located between 1000 and 1500 ft beyond the departure end of the runway along the runway centerline. The elevation transmitter is normally located 400 ft from the runway centerline near the approach threshold.

(d) Transportation Requirements.

•By air: 1 C-130.

•By road: 1 M-35/M-923.

(e) Minimal Mission Capability and Setup Timing. The system requires 4 personnel. Currently, there is no manpower assigned to the system. Special Operations Command uses combat controllers (operations section) to install the system, and the ANG has embedded the system into the TACAN UTC (maintenance section). The system can be operational within 1.5 hours.

Table E-3 lists communications capabilities provided by specific organizations and ATC systems.

Table E-3 Communications Capabilities

ORGANIZATION	SYSTEMS	COMM CAPABILITY
USSOCOM (STT)	PROVIDE VFR/LIMITED IFR MMLS PRECISION LANDING CAPABILITY FOR MLS EQUIPPED C-130/C-17	UHF AM/FM/VOICE/DATA SECURE, VHF AM/FM/VOICE /DATA/SECURE, HF SECURE/VOICE/DATA, SATCOM-TACSAT/SECURE, IMARSAT, HAVE QUICK, SINGARS
USAF (COMBAT COMM)	MRC-144 L+45 MIN INITIAL CONTROL TOWER LIMITED VFR	HAV EQUICK UHF/VHF/HF
	TSW-7 L+16 HOURS MOBILE CONTROL TOWER	5 UHF/4 VHF 3 LANDLINES 3 DIRECT
	TPN-19 L+36 HOURS MOBILE RAPCON	HAVE QUICK 9 UHF/5 VHF 3 LANDLINES 13 DIRECT
ANG (ATCS)	MPN-14 L+24 HOURS MOBILE RAPCON TSW-7	HAVE QUICK 7 UHF/5 VHF 6 LANDLINES 1 DIRECT
ARMY	TSQ-198 VFR SERVICE	1 UHF HAVE QUICK/VOICE/DATA (SECURE) 1 VHF HAVE QUICK/VOICE/DATE (SECURE) 1 HF VOICE/DATA (SECURE) 1 FM SINGARS (SECURE)
	TSQ-71B VFR/IFR ATS SERVICE PRECISION APPROACHES	3 UHF 3 VHF 2 FM SINGARS (SECURE)
	TSC-61B ENROUTE FLIGHT FOLLOWING AIRSPACE INTEGRATION	3 VHF 3 UHF 3 SINGARS (SECURE) 1 HF
	TSW-7A VFR/IFR ATS TOWER SERVICE	3 VHF 3 UHF 3 SINGARS (SECURE) 1 HF
USMC	MMT	2 UHF 2 VHF 1 HF
	MATCD* EACH CCS	2 VHF-FM/HF-AM SSB 8 UHF-AM/TADIL-C 3 VHF-AM 10 TELEPHONE LINES
	MATCD CONTROL TOWER	1 VHF-FM 1 VHF-FM/HF-AM SSB 5 UHF 3 VHF-AM 10 TELEPHONE LINES
* NOTE: WHEN DEPLOYED IN DUAL-SHELTER CONFIGURATION, CAPABILITY DOUBLES		

Appendix F

NAVY TACTICAL AIR CONTROL SQUADRON DUTY POSITIONS

1. Background

This appendix describes the duties of the primary air operations positions within the tactical air control squadron (TACRON) and its detachments.

2. Tactical Air Controller

The tactical air controller is the senior officer in the tactical air control center (TACC), responsible for management and execution of air operations within and around the amphibious objective area (AOA). Except in very large operations, most detachment officers in charge (OICs) will fill both tactical actions officer (TAO) and tactical air controller billets. The OIC receives notification of and initiates search and rescue (SAR) missions, notifying the amphibious squadron (PHIBRON) staff of fixed- and rotary-wing assets available. The OIC determines the need for rescue combat air patrol (RESCAP). The OIC also coordinates the use of airspace coordination areas. For underway operations, the tactical air controller has overall responsibility for TACRON operations. There are 3 main areas that are managed by the tactical air controller and the subordinates: helicopter coordination, air warfare, and close air support (CAS). Each of these 3 areas is headed by a coordinator to ensure safety and mission accomplishment and all are functions of the TACC.

3. Air Support Coordinator (ASC)

The ASC supervises the air support control section (ASCS) and advises supporting arms coordinator (SAC) on the use of CAS aircraft.

4. Assistant Air Support Coordinator (AASC)

The AASC is responsible to ASC. Functions of the AASC—

(1) Exercises supervision and direction over all aircraft assigned to the CAS section.

(2) Monitors performance, fuel, and weaponry of CAS aircraft.

(3) Recommends to ASC units that are best suited to carry out assigned missions.

(4) Assigns aircraft for strike and support missions.

(5) Advises ASC on the execution status of air support missions.

(6) Directs orbiting, air refueling, and/or return to base (RTB).

(7) Aids ASC in coordination and use of airspace coordination area(s).

5. TACC Supervisor

Functions of the TACC supervisor—

(1) Ensures all air traffic services provided are safe, orderly, and expeditious.

(2) Monitors all air operations and services provided in the AOA.

(3) Qualifies for all positions in the ATC section.

(4) Responsible for the safe and expeditious handling of all aircraft operating within the AOA.

(5) Supervises the tactical air control section.

(6) Responsible for tactical air traffic controllers and tactical air direction controllers.

(7) Responsible for keeping the TAC and TACC watch officers informed regarding all aspects of TACC operations, from helicopter coordination to SAR operations.

6. Tactical Air Traffic Controller

The tactical air traffic controller is responsible for separation and coordination of air traffic during approach to, operations within, and retirement from the AOA/AOR. This function is performed normally under radar/positive airspace management conditions. The tactical air traffic controller, with the concurrence of TACC supervisor, assigns entry, holding, and exit points for all aircraft. The tactical air traffic controller identifies and checks in all aircraft entering the AOA and passes the following: weather, diverts, deconfliction information, changes to the expected route, altitude information, and traffic. The tactical air traffic controller separates and controls all inbound and outbound aircraft that effects handover to the tactical air director (TAD), air intercept controller, air warfare commander (AWC), or to a point clear of the AOA. The tactical air traffic controller coordinates with air warfare coordinator all combat air patrol (CAP) arrival/departure missions. Also the tactical air traffic controller coordinates airspace usage for mission deconfliction and route and altitude for safety, separation, deconfliction, and efficiency. The tactical air traffic controller section is responsible for tactical ATC and for dissemination of all tactical information to aircraft that check into the AOA. The tactical air controller will pass control over to the TAD.

7. TAD

The TAD coordinates with the tactical air controller as required to ensure the safe, efficient, and orderly control of tactical air traffic. TACRONs normally plan for manning of 2 TAD positions in operations of any size. These controllers are assigned and report to the AASC, but the actual operation of coordinating the movement of strike aircraft is tactical air traffic controller-to-TAD direct. Duties include— providing separation and direction of aircraft assigned, coordinating and deconflicting traffic situations as required, and coordinating and directing assistance during SAR and emergency operations.

The TAD passes control of CAS mission flights to the TACP for individual tasks. The TAD responds directly to tasking provided by the ASC. The ASC ensures that aircraft carrying the proper ordnance are assigned appropriate targets. This requires a thorough knowledge of the different types and uses of ordnance and also air delivery methods. The ASC passes the target location to the TAD, who directs the aircraft to assigned targets. Upon completion of the aircraft mission, the aircraft checks in with the TAD, who receives the battle damage assessment and passes this information to the ASC to determine if additional aircraft are needed to ensure target destruction.

8. Helicopter Coordinator (HC)

A typical amphibious assault will employ multiple waves of helicopters. The HC is responsible for the coordination of all helicopter traffic within the assigned AOA. The HC passes direction to the helicopter direction center/air operations control center (HDC/AOCC), who provides direct radar control of the assault force helicopters. HDC/AOCC is a function of every general purpose amphibious assault ship/multipurpose amphibious assault ship (LHA/LHD) and amphibious assault ship, landing platform helicopter (LPH) within the US Navy and provides ATC to the helicopters. The HC utilizes the console for monitoring the progress of the aircraft ashore. It is also the HC's function to prepare and ensure the air tasking order is carried out and disseminated.

9. AWC

The air warfare section is manned by an AWC, who is responsible for ensuring every air contact within the area is positively identified. In the event of a hostile contact, it is the AWC's function to destroy the threat with all the assets that are available. Directly under the AWC is the air intercept controller supervisor who assists the AWC in the employment of fighter aircraft and surface to air systems through use of a senior OS who is assigned to the position of air warfare console operator.

TACTICAL AIR CONTROL SQUADRON REQUIRED OPERATIONAL CAPABILITIES (ROC)

1. Background.

This appendix contains detailed information on the required operational capabilities of the TACRONs.

2. Air Warfare (AW)

Functions of AW are—

a. Providing air defense in coopera-tion with other forces, including coordinat-ing air defense planning as AWC for battle group convoy amphibious operations.

b. Providing air defense of a geo-graphic area (zone) in cooperation with other forces.

c. Engaging air targets during battle group operations in cooperation with other forces.

d. Controlling combat air patrol.

(1) Supporting/conducting air intercept missions against multiple aircraft and subsurface, surface, or air launched missiles.

(2) Providing continuous multiple air intercept control capability.

e. Coordinating the overall conduct of AW operations with all other warfare requirements of the amphibious task force (ATF) commander; allocating air assets as required to counter threats to the ATF.

Note: Group 2 TACRONs are not manned to support the AW commander.

3. Amphibious Warfare (AMW)

Functions of AMW are—

a. Providing air control and coordi-nation of air operations in an amphibious objective area (AOA) and in transit.

(1) Providing ATC, controlling all air support aircraft, and coordinating helicopter operations in an AOA and in transit.

(2) Providing coordination of AW, surface warfare (SUW) and under sea warfare (USW) air assets for protection of the force in an AOA.

(3) Controlling air search and rescue (SAR) operations in AOA. Coordinating air assets in the AOA with supporting arms to provide safe, coordinated action.

b. Providing for air operations in support of amphibious operations.

(1) Controlling aircraft under all conditions of active jamming.

(2) Providing air strike control to direct or assist attack aircraft.

c. Conducting tactical recovery of aircraft and personnel (TRAP).

4. Surface Warfare

Functions of Surface Warfare are—

a. Supporting surface ship defense of geographical area in cooperation with other forces.

b. Providing for air operations in support of surface attack operations.

Providing air strike control to direct or assist attack aircraft.

c. Performing duties of the aircraft control unit (ACU) for aircraft involved in SUW operations.

5. Under Sea Warfare

Functions of USW are—

Providing for USW defense in support of amphibious operations

6. Command, Control, and Communications (C3)

Functions of C3 are—

a. Coordinating and controlling the operations of the task organization or functional force to carry out assigned missions.

b. Coordinating the reconnaissance of multiple surface, subsurface and/or air contacts.

c. Functioning as AWC for force or sector.

d. Functioning as on-scene commander for a search and rescue (SAR) operation.

e. Establishing a tactical air control center (TACC) and/or tactical air direction center (TADC) as appropriate to support the tactical air officer (TAO); TACC will control and/or coordinate all fixed-wing air assets within the AOA and in transit.

f. Establishing a helicopter coordination section (HCS) to support the TAO; HCS will coordinate helicopter operations within the AOA and in transit during multideck operations.

g. Controlling close air support aircraft in support of amphibious operations; controlling function will include coordination with other supporting arms.

h. Coordinating and controlling air SAR operations in the AOA.

i. Functioning as one or more of the following coordinators for force or sector: air element coordinator/Light Airborne Multipurpose System (LAMPS) element coordinator (LEC).

j. Assisting in the planning of AW, SUW, and USW for the coordination of air operations in the AOA and transit.

7. Fleet Support Operations (FSO)

FSO supports/conducts SAR operations in a combat/noncombat environment. Functions of FSO are—

a. Supporting/conducting combat/noncombat SAR operations by fixed or rotary wing aircraft.

b. Acquiring and displaying distress data.

c. Reporting situation assessment.

d. Coordinating SAR operations.

e. Conducting multiunit SAR operation.

8. Intelligence

Functions of intelligence are—

a. Supporting/conducting unarmed reconnaissance (weather, visual, BDA, etc.).

b. Supporting the processing of surveillance and reconnaissance information.

c. Supporting the dissemination of surveillance and reconnaissance information.

d. Operating a contingency planning cell to support fleet commanders.

9. Mobility

Functions of mobility are—

a. Operating from a ship with a helicopter platform.

b. Operating from a ship capable of supporting air control activities in support of amphibious operations.

c. Conducting operations ashore in climatic extremes ranging from cold weather to tropical to desert environments.

10. Noncombat Operation

Noncombat operations are—

a. Providing disaster assistance and evacuation and staff ATC facilities ashore.

b. Supporting providing for the evacuation of noncombatant personnel in areas of civil or international crisis.

(1) Supporting/conducting helicopter/boat evacuation of noncombatant personnel as directed by higher authority from areas of civil or international crisis.

(2) Supporting/conducting day/night rotary-wing aircraft operations.

(3) Supporting/conducting rotary-wing aircraft flight operations during all emission control (EMCON) conditions.

c. Conducting counter narcotic and other law enforcement support operations in conjunction with other forces. Also conducting operations with Coast Guard units.

d. Detecting and monitoring suspicious air contacts.

11. Strike Warfare (STW)

Functions of STW are—

a. Supporting and conducting air strikes by supporting/participating in conventional air strike operations or major air strike operations under all conditions of readiness.

b. Providing for air operations in support of air strike operations by providing control of all aircraft en route to and returning from assigned missions.

Appendix H

SPECIAL TACTICS SQUADRON (STS) MISSION TASKS

This appendix contains a comprehensive list of the mission tasks that special tactics forces are required to perform.

a. Conduct on-site assessments of as many potential target sites, assault zones (AZs), ISB/FSB/FOB locations as possible in the area of interest.

b. Collect, collate, and provide sufficient assault zone and airfield survey data to support timely mission planning requirements.

c. Develop and provide precise, to scale computer enhanced target/assault zone/ airfield diagrams, photographs and other survey products as necessary to support mission planning requirements.

d. Establish and control assault zones or conduct turnover operations without interruption of terminal guidance services, at times and locations established in the mission OPORD.

e. Conduct fire support and/or laser target designation operations as required in support of R&S team and/or follow-on forces movements/operations.

f. Conduct and relay limited weather observations as required to support detailed mission planning and follow-on forces requirements.

g. Conduct demolition operations to clear obstacles from assault zones required to support follow-on forces movements/ operations.

h. Provide real-time intelligence/ information on AZs.

i. Define operational parameters of AZs based on number/type of aircraft, procedures, ground plans, physical and environmental characteristics of target zone(s).

j. Formulate aircraft/ground movement and parking plan in concert with the land component commander tactical requirements.

k. Determine requirements for NAVAIDS, beacons, portable radar equipment, and assault zone lighting to assist aircraft operations in a VMC/limited IMC operational environment.

l. Provide continuous tactical interface with ground forces command elements to coordinate air movement, provide timely assessments, and monitor ground movement to ensure the safe and expeditious flow of air traffic in concert with the ground tactical plan.

m. Conduct SAR security team operations with identified ground force security element using available rotary wing assets IAW applicable standing operating procedures (SOP) and mission CSAR plan.

n. Provide on-scene extrication, triage, emergency medical treatment, and en route medical treatment during extraction IAW established medical protocols and SOP.

o. Utilize identified CSAR platforms and plans to locate, authenticate, and recover distressed personnel as quickly as the tactical situation and safety of flight considerations permit.

p. Control fixed- and rotary-wing CAS operations, to include AC-130 gunship operations, using prebriefed procedures and appropriate SOP while minimizing collateral damage to friendly personnel or structures

Appendix I

SAMPLE AIR TRAFFIC CONTROL HANDOVER CHECKLISTS

SAMPLE ONE

1. Control # _____

2. Mission # _____ a. Change # _____ b. Ref # _____

3. Frequency (Primary/Back Up):

    a. UHF   (P)_____   (A)_____

    b. VHF   (P)_____   (A)_____

    c. HF   (P)_____   (A)_____

    d. FM   (P)_____   (A)_____

    e. SATCOM (UP) _____   (DN)_____

4. Threat _____

5. Fld Elev_____ ft MSL

6. TD Zone Elev _____ ft MSL

7. Dimensions   L   W

    a. RWY   ____ ft   ____ ft

    b. TXWY   ____ ft   ____ ft

    c. OVRN   ____ ft   ____ ft

    d. HELIPD   ____ ft   ____ ft

8. Usable Txwy   Yes (Y)   No (N)

9. Active Rwy _____/_____   Runway Crossing Points (RCP) _____

10. MOG: a. C-130____   b. C-141____   c. C-5 ____   d. MC-130 ____

        e. C-17____ f. HELO ____   g. Other_____

11. Parking Spots
    a. Locations
        (1) Fixed-Wing_____

        (2) HELO_____

12. Marshallers Req: a. Fixed-Wing Y N b. HELO Y N

13. Hot Cargo Area   Y N Location _____

14. Refueling Points   Y N Location_____

15. Arming Areas   Y   N Location_____

16. Average on load time _____ min

17. Average off load time _____ min

18. Obstacles on Airfield: Y N

    a. Trees   Y N _____ ft

    b. Wires   Y N _____ ft

    c. Houses   Y N _____ ft

    d. Personnel   Y N _____ ft

    e. Ditches   Y N _____ ft

    f. Terrain   Y N _____ ft

    g. Poles   Y N _____ ft

19. Obstacles in Class D airspace: Y N

    a. Trees   Y N _____ ft

    b. Wires   Y N _____ ft

    c. Houses   Y N _____ ft

    d. Personnel   Y N _____ ft

    e. Ditches   Y N _____ ft

    f. Terrain   Y N _____ ft

    g. Poles   Y N _____ ft

20. Blind Spots

    a. Visual_____

    b. Radio_____

21. NAVAIDS

    a. TACAN   G   R

        (1) Location _____

        (2) Frequency _____

        (3) Power Source _____

    b. MMLS   G   R

        (1) Location _____

        (2) Frequency _____

        (3) Power Source _____

    c. ZM   G   R

        (1) Location _____

        (2) Frequency _____

        (3) Power Source _____

    d. ILS   G   R

        (1) Location _____

        (2) Frequency _____

        (3) Power Source _____

    e. NDB   G   R

        (1) Location _____

        (2) Frequency _____

        (3) Power Source _____

22. Nonradar Handoff Procedures

    a. HDG _____

    b. Handoff

        (1) Time _____ (hhmm)

        (2) Fix _____

        (3) Alt _____

        (4) Frequency _____

        (5) Location _____

        (6) C/S _____

23. Airfield Lighting:

    a. AMP1 (AFI 13-217)

    b. AMP2 (RCL)

    c. AMP3 (Box 1)

    d. AMP4 (B/O)

    e. None

24. SR _____

25. SS _____

26. TERPS Y N

27. Reporting Points

    a. LOC _____

    b. ALT _____

    e. PATTERN_____

28. Holding Points VFR

    a. LOC _____

    b. ALT _____

    c. PATTERN_____

29. Holding Points IFR

    a. LOC _____

    b. ALT _____

    c. PATTERN _____

30. Traffic Patterns

    a. Left

    b. Right

    c. Straight In

    d. OVHD

    e. Other _____

31. Jettison Area

    a. LOC _____

    b. ALT _____

32. Bailout Area

    a. LOC _____

    b. ALT _____

33. Fuel Dump Area

    a. LOC _____

    b. ALT _____

34. NOTAMS _____

35. Current Traffic _____

36. Projected Traffic _____

37. Alternate Airfields _____

38. Friendly Forces:

Agency	C/S	MGRS Location	Freq	Key Tape
Departing ATC	_____	_____	_____	_____
Arty Column	_____	_____	_____	_____
FDC	_____	_____	_____	_____
Air Base Defense	_____	_____	_____	_____
ALCE	_____	_____	_____	_____
ALCC	_____	_____	_____	_____
AFSOB	_____	_____	_____	_____
Crash/Rescue	_____	_____	_____	_____
Close Air Support	_____	_____	_____	_____
MEDEVAC	_____	_____	_____	_____
TOC	_____	_____	_____	_____
US Army Main Forces	_____	_____	_____	_____
US Marines Forces	_____	_____	_____	_____
US Navy Main Fleet	_____	_____	_____	_____
Allied Forces	_____	_____	_____	_____
ABCCC	_____	_____	_____	_____
AWACS	_____	_____	_____	_____

39. Traffic Information: (Use DELTA Three message format flow tasking)

40. Weather: (Use GOLF message format)

41. Artillery: (Use HOTEL One message format)

42. Remarks:

_____

_____

_____

43. Passed To _____ DTG _____Z Initials____
                                      (dd/hhmm/mm/yy)

CHANGE #_____

   Passed To _____ DTG _____Z Initials____
                                      (dd/hhmm/mm/yy)

NOTES

SAMPLE TWO

1. Airfield Name: _____

2. Airfield Location: _____   lat/long: _____/_____

3. ICAO Identifier: _____

4. Airfield Frequencies: (P) UHF/VHF   (S) UHF/VHF

   ATIS   _____/_____   _____/_____

   Approach Control   _____/_____   _____/_____

   Tower Control   _____/_____   _____/_____

   Ground Control   _____/_____   _____/_____

   Clearence Delivery _____/_____   _____/_____

   Base Operations   _____/_____   _____/_____

   SAR   _____/_____   _____/_____

   WX Metro   _____/_____   _____/_____

5. Airfield Diagram:

6. Usable Runways: ___/___/___/___

7. Usable Taxiways: ___/___/___/___/___/___

8. Dimensions: Length   Width   Composition   PCN

    Runway   _____ft   _____ft   _____   ___/___/___/___
                    _____ft   _____ft   _____   ___/___/___/___
                    _____ft   _____ft   _____   ___/___/___/___
                    _____ft   _____ft   _____   ___/___/___/___
    Taxiway   _____ft   _____ft   _____   ___/___/___/___
                    _____ft   _____ft   _____   ___/___/___/___
                    _____ft   _____ft   _____   ___/___/___/___
                    _____ft   _____ft   _____   ___/___/___/___
                    _____ft   _____ft   _____   ___/___/___/___
                    _____ft   _____ft   _____   ___/___/___/___
                    _____ft   _____ft   _____   ___/___/___/___
    Helipad   _____ft   _____ft   _____   ___/___/___/___
                    _____ft   _____ft   _____   ___/___/___/___
                    _____ft   _____ft   _____   ___/___/___/___
    AV-8B Pad   _____ft   _____ft   _____   ___/___/___/___
                    _____ft   _____ft   _____   ___/___/___/___
                    _____ft   _____ft   _____   ___/___/___/___

9. Traffic Pattern: Entry Point   Altitude   Point of Descent

    Left   _____   _____   _____
    Right   _____   _____   _____
    Straight-in   _____   _____   _____
    Overhead   _____   _____   _____
    Other   _____   _____   _____

10. Pattern Altitude:

    Turbo-Jet   _____   Altitude Remarks:
    Propeller-Driven _____
    Helo   _____

11. NAVAIDs: Location   /Frequency   /Power Source
               Lat/Long

    NDB   _____/_____/_____
    VOR   _____/_____/_____
    TACAN   _____/_____/_____
    VORTAC   _____/_____/_____
    MLS   _____/_____/_____
    ILS   _____/_____/_____
    GPS   _____/_____/_____
    VASI   _____/_____/_____
    ASR   _____/_____/_____
    PAR   _____/_____/_____

12. Hot Cargo Area: Y___   N___

13. Refueling Points: Y___   N___

     Location _____

14. Arming/Dearming Area: Y___   N___

     Location _____

15. Parking Locations/Spots/Restrictions:

     Fixed-Wing   _____
                            _____
                            _____

     Rotary-Wing   _____
                            _____
                            _____

     VIP/VAL   _____
                            _____
                            _____

16. Obstacles on Airfield: Y___   N___

     Trees   Y___   N___   _____ft
     Wires   Y___   N___   _____ft
     Houses   Y___   N___   _____ft
     Personnel   Y___   N___   _____ft
     Ditches   Y___   N___   _____ft
     Terrain   Y___   N___   _____ft
     Poles   Y___   N___   _____ft

17. Blind Spots:

     Visual   _____
     Radio   _____

18. Nonradar Procedures:

     Heading _____
     Handoff
          Time   _____
          Fix   _____
          Altitude   _____
          Frequency _____
          Location   _____

19. TERPS: Y ___   N ___

20. Reporting Points: #1   #2   #3   #4

    Location   _____   _____   _____   _____
    Altitude   _____   _____   _____   _____

21. Holding Points VFR:

    Location   _____   _____   _____   _____
    Altitude   _____   _____   _____   _____
    Pattern   _____   _____   _____   _____

22. Holding Points IFR:

    Location   _____   _____   _____   _____
    Altitude   _____   _____   _____   _____
    Pattern   _____   _____   _____   _____

23. Bailout Area:

    Location   _____   _____   _____   _____
    Altitude   _____   _____   _____   _____

24. Jettison Area:

    Location   _____   _____   _____   _____
    Altitude   _____   _____   _____   _____

25. Fuel Dump Area:

    Location   _____   _____   _____   _____
    Altitude   _____   _____   _____   _____

26. Alternate/Divert Airfields Information:

        Name/TACAN/Heading /Distance/Elevation/Fuel/Longest/APCH/Twr
        Channel from airfield (NM)   Runway Freq Freq
                NAVAIDS

____/_____/____/____/____/_____/____/_____/____/____
____/_____/____/____/____/_____/____/_____/____/____
____/_____/____/____/____/_____/____/_____/____/____
____/_____/____/____/____/_____/____/_____/____/____
____/_____/____/____/____/_____/____/_____/____/____
____/_____/____/____/____/_____/____/_____/____/____
____/_____/____/____/____/_____/____/_____/____/____
____/_____/____/____/____/_____/____/_____/____/____

27. Weather:

    Wind: Prevailing _____/_____   Surface _____/_____

    VSBY   ____Mi

    Ice   Y__   N__

    Wet   Y__   N__   Rain/Snow

    Breaking Action

         Good__   Fair__   Poor__   NIL__   UNK __

    Other:

28. Remarks:

REFERENCES

Joint

Joint Pub 1-02, *DOD Dictionary of Military and Associated Terms*

Joint Pub 3-52, *Joint Airspace in the Combat Zone*

Joint Pub 3-56.1, *Command and Control for Joint Air Operations*

Multiservice

Multiservice Procedures for Integrated Combat Airspace Command and Control (ICAC2)

Multiservice Procedures for the Theater Air Ground System (TAGS)

Army

FM 1-120, *Army Air Traffic Services Contingency and Combat Operations*

FM 1-303, *Air Traffic Control Facility Operations and Training*

FM 24-24, *Signal Data References: Signal Equipment*

FM 100-13, *Battlefield Coordination Detachment (BCD)*

FM 101-5-1, *Operational Terms and Graphics*

Equipment Description Sheets from United States Army Aviation Center, Directoate of Combat Development (DCD), Ft Rucker, AL

US Army Operations Concept for Air Traffic Services, 6 May 96

USAAVNC Pam 525-5, *Aviation in Force XXI Operations,* 2 Jan 96

Vision for Force XXI Air Traffic Services, DA/ODCSOPS, 14 Feb 96

US Army Air Traffic Control Activity Mission Briefing, 21 Jun 96

TRADOC Pamphlet 525-72, *Army Airspace Command and Control (A2C2)*

ATS Concept Briefing, United States Army Aviation Center, 26 Jun 95

TAIS briefing slides, DCD, Ft Rucker, AL, 10 Jul 95

Information Paper, *Lack of Army Airspace Command and Control (A2C2) and Joint Communication Automation (Airspace Integration) Capabilities,* United States Army Aviation Center, Directorate of Combat Development (DCD), 15 May 96

TAIS Operational Requirements Document, 5 May 95

ATNAVICS Operational Requirements Document, 20 Sep 94

TTCS Operational Requirements Document, 23 Nov 92

Information Paper, *ATC Tactical and Fixed Base Modernization,* United States Army Aviation Center, Directorate of Combat Development (DCD), 1 Jan 96

Information Paper, *ATNAVICS,* United States Army Aviation Center, Directorate of Combat Development (DCD), 1 Jul 96

Faxed briefing slides, 29 ATS Group, National Guard, Glen Arm, MD

HQDA ADCSOPS-FD, *ATC Worldwide Organizational and Management Assesment*

Marine Corps

MCWP 3-25.8, *Marine Air Traffic Control Detachment Handbook*

E-mail from MCCDC on MACS/MATCD organizational breakdown and unit locations

Navy

Fax documents from Tactical Air Control Group 1, NAB Coronedo, San Diego, CA, on mission, squadron manning, squadron organization, and squadron detachment positions for underway operations.

Fax documents from Tactical Air Control Group 2, NAB Little Creek, Norfolk VA, on the organization of a group, squadron, detachment, the various supporting sections, detailed descriptions of positions within those organizations, amphibious ATC equipment listing, the projected operational environment and required operational capabilities for tactical air control squadrons.

Air Force

AFDD 2-1.7, *Airspace Control in the Combat Zone (DRAFT)*

AFI 13-AO, Volume 3, *Operational Procedures—Air Operations Center*

AFI 13-203, *Air Traffic Control*

AFMAN 11-225, *United States Standard Flight Inspection Manual*

Fax from the 23 STS, Hurlburt Field, FL, concerning mission statement, group organization, and equipment breakdown

Manpower Force Element Listing, 23 STS, Hurlburt Field, FL

Strategic Plan, 23 STS, Hurlburt Field, FL, 25 Mar 96

USAF Program Guidance Letter, *Organization of Air Force Deployable Command, Control, Communications, and Computers (C4) and Deployable Air Traffic Control and Landing Systems (DATCALS) Force Structure*, 1 Jun 96

HQ ACC/DOFR DATCALS Brief, *Wartime Mission / Deployment Strategy / Equipment and Capabilities*

Final Mission Need Statement, *Air Traffic Control and Landing Systems (ATCALS)*, HQ AFFSA/XXR, 23 Jul 96

Other

HQ ACC/CV, Memo, *Joint Air Traffic Control (JATC) Comparative Analysis*, not dated, approximate date, Apr to May 96

HQ USAF/XO, Memo, *Deployable Air Traffic Control and Landing System (ATCALS) Comparative Analysis*, 16 Apr 96

GLOSSARY

PART I—ABBREVIATIONS AND ACRONYMS

A

A2C2	Army airspace command and control
AADC	area air defense commander
AAGS	Army air-ground system
AASC	assistant air support coordinator
AASC	Army area signal center (USA)
AASLT	air assault
ABCCC	airborne battlefield command and control center
ABCS	Army Battle Command System
abn	airborne
A/C	aircraft
AC	alternating current, active component
ACA	airspace control authority
ACC	Air Combat Command; air component commander; area coordination center
ACE	aviation combat element (MAGTF); airborne command element (USAF); air combat element (NATO); Allied Command Europe
ACLS	automatic carrier landing system
ACM	airspace control measure
ACO	airspace control order
ACP	airspace control plan
ACS	airspace control system
ACU	aircraft control unit
AD	active duty
ADA	air defense artillery
ADF	automatic direction finding
ADVON	advanced echelon or cadre
AETC	Air Education and Training Command
AF	Air Force
AFATDS	Advanced Field Artillery Tactical Data System
AFB	Air Force Base
AFCC	Air Force Component Commander
AFDC	Air Force Doctrine Center
AFFOR	Air Force forces
AFFSA	Air Force Flight Standards Agency
AFI	Air Force Instruction
AFM	Air Force Manual
AFMAN	Air Force Manual
AFMC	Air Force Materiel Command
AFSOB	Air Force Special Operations Base
AFSOC	Air Force special operations component
AGOS	Air Ground Operations School (Hurlburt Field)
AIC	air intercept controller, airspace information center
AIS	airspace information service
AL	Alabama

ALB	airland battle
ALB-F	Airland battle-future
ALCC	airlift control center
ALCE	airlift control element
ALS	all-weather landing subsystem
ALSA	Air Land Sea Application Center
alt	altitude
AM	amplitude modulating
AMC	Air Mobility Command
AMLS	airspace management liaison section
AMP	airfield marking pattern
AMW	amphibious warfare
ANCOC	Advanced Noncommissioned Officer Course
ANG	Air National Guard
ANGB	Air National Guard Base
AO	area of operations
AOA	amphibious objective area
AOC	air operations center (USAF)
AOCC	air operations control center
AOF	airfield operations flight
AOR	area of responsibility
apch	approach
APG	Air Procedures Guide, Aviator Procedures Guide
AR	Army Regulation; Arkansas
ARATC	advanced radar air traffic control
AREC	air resource element coordinator
ARFOR	Army forces
ARG	amphibious ready group
arm	armor
ARTEP	Army Training and Evaluation Program
arty	artillery
ARW	air reconnaissance wing
ASC	air support coordinator
ASC(A)	assault support coordinator (airborne)
ASCS	air support control section (USN)
ASI	additional skill identifier (USA)
aslt	assault
ASR	area surveillance radar
ATA	airport traffic area
ATC	air traffic control
ATCCS	Army Tactical Command and Control System
ATCS	air traffic control section
ATF	amphibious task force
ATIS	automatic terminal information service
ATNAVICS	air traffic navigation, integration and coordination system
ATO	air tasking order
ATS	air traffic service; assign terminal service; assign secondary traffic channels
ATV	all terrain vehicle
auth	authorized
AW	air warfare; Air Wing
AWACS	Airborne Warning and Control System

AWC	air warfare commander
AWS	air warfare section
AZ	assault zone; Arizona

B

B/O	black out
BAS	battlefield automated systems
BCD	battlefield coordination detachment (USA)
BDA	bomb or battle damage assessment
BDZ	base defense zone
bn	battalion
BNCOC	Basic Noncommissioned Officer Course (USA)
BOS	base operating support
BSC	Battle Staff Course (USA)

C

C2	command and control
C3	command, control, and communications
C3I	command, control, communications and intelligence
C4	command, control, communications, and computers
C4ISR	command, control, communications, computers, intelligence, surveillance and reconnaissance
C/S	call sign
CA	coordinating altitude; California
CAC	combined arms center (USA)
CAC2S	common aviation command and control system
CAIC	corps airspace information center
CAP	combat air patrol
CAS	close air support
CATCC	carrier air traffic control center
CATCO	chief, air traffic control operations
CATF	commander, amphibious task force
cav	cavalry
CBR	chemical, biological, radiological
CC	commander
CCG	combat communications group
CCS	control and communications subsystem
CCT	combat control team
CDC	combat direction center
cdr	commander
CE	command element
CGSC	Command and General Staff College (USA)
CINC	commander in chief
CJCS	Chairman of the Joint Chiefs of Staff
CMF	career management field
CNO	Chief of Naval Operations
cntrl	control
CO	Colorado
co	company
COA	course of action

comm	communications
COMMZ	communications zone
COMNAV	communications/navigational
COMSEC	communications security
CONUS	continental United States
coord	coordination
CRAF	Civil Reserve Air Fleet
CRC	control and reporting center
CRE	control reporting element
crs	course
CRT	cathode ray tube
CSAR	combat search and rescue
CT	counterterrorism
CTAPS	contingency theater automated planning system (USAF)
CTF	combined task force
CTO	Certified Training Operator
CTOC	corp tactical operations center
CV	aircraft carrier
CVBG	carrier battle group
CVN	aircraft carrier nuclear
CWC	composite warfare commander

D

DA	Department of the Army; direct action
DAIC	Division Airspace Information Center
DAMS	Dynamic Airspace Management System (USA)
DARR	Department of the Army Regional Representative
DASC	direct air support center (USMC)
DASC(A)	direct air support center (airborne)
DATCALS	deployable air traffic control and landing systems
DCP	director of combat plans
DCSOPS	Deputy Chief of Staff Operations
DE	directed energy
det	detachment; detainee
div	Division
DME	distance measuring equipment
DOD	Department of Defense
DS	direct support
DTG	date time group
DTLOM	doctrine, training, leader development, organization and materiel
DTOC	divison tactical operations center
DTS	Defense Transportation System
DZ	drop zone

E

E1	Private (USA)/Airman Basic (USAF)/Seaman Recruit (USN)/ Private (USMC)
E2	Private (USA)/Airman (USAF)/Seaman Apprentice (USN)/Private First Class (USMC)
E3	Private First Class (USA)/Airman First Class (USAF)/Seamna (USN)/

	Lance Corporal (USMC)
E4	Corporal or Specialist (USA)/Senior Airman (USAF)/Petty Officer Third Class (USN)/Corporal (USMC)
E5	Sergeant (USA)/Staff Sergeant (USAF)/Petty Officer Second Class (USN)/Sergeant (USMC)
E6	Staff Sergeant (USA)/Technical Sergeant (USAF)/Petty Officer First Class (USN)/Staff Sergeant (USMC)
E7	Sergeant First Class (USA)/Master Sergeant (USAF)/Chief Petty Officer (USN)/Gunnery Sergeant (USMC)
E8	First Sergeant or Master Sergeant (USA)/Senior Master Sergeant (USAF)/Senior Chief Petty Officer (USN)/First Sergeant or Master Sergeant (USMC)
E9	Command Sergeant Major or Sergeant Major (USA)/Chief Master Sergeant (USAF)/Command Master Chief Petty Officer or Master Chief Petty Officer (USN)/Sergeant Major or Master Gunnery Sergeant (USMC)
EAC	echelons above corps
elev	elevation
EMCON	emission control
EP	electronic protection
ETVS	enhanced terminal voice switch
EW	electronic warfare
EW/C	early warning and control

F

FA	field artillery
FAA	Federal Aviation Administration
FAAD	forward area air defense
FAADS	Forward Air Defense System (USA)
FAAH	Federal Aviation Administration Handbook
FAC	forward air controller
FAC(A)	forward air controller (airborne)
FAR	Federal Aviation Regulation
FARP	forward arming and refueling point
FASFAC	Fleet Air Control and Surveillance Facility (USN)
FAWC	Fleet Air Warfare Commander (USN)
FCC	flight coordination center
FDC	fire direction center
FEBA	forward edge of the battle area
FID	foreign internal defense
FL	Florida
fld	field
FM	frequency modulation; field manual
FMF	Fleet Marine Force
FOB	forward operations base, forward operating base (USMC)
FOC	Flight Operations Center
FORSCOM	US Army Forces Command
FSB	forward staging base, forward support battalion
FSC	fire support coordinator
FSO	fleet support operations
ft	fort; feet; foot

FTP	facility training program
FUE	first unit equipped
FW	fighter wing

G

G-3	Army or Marine Corps component operations staff officer (Army division or higher, Marine Corps aircraft wing or division or higher staff)
GA	Georgia
GBAD	ground based air defense
GCA	ground controlled approach
GCP	ground commander's pointer
GE	Germany
gen	generator
GFC	ground forces commander
Gp	group
GPS	global positioning system
GS	general support

H

HA	humanitarian assistance
HC	helicopter coordinator
HCS	helicopter coordination section
HDC	helicopter direction center
hdg	heading
helipd	helicopter pad
HELO	helicopter
HF	high frequency
HI	Hawaii
HLZ	helicopter landing zone
HMMWV	high mobility multipurpose wheeled vehicle
HQ	headquarters
HST	helicopter support team
Hz	hertz

I

IADS	Integrated Air Defense System
IAP	International Airport
IAW	in accordance with
ICAO	International Civil Aviation Organization
ID	Infantry Division
id	identification
IFF	identification, friend or foe
IFR	instrument flight rules
IL	Illinois
ILS	instrument landing system
IMC	instrument meteorological conditions
IN	Indiana

inf	infantry
intel	intelligence
ISB	intermediate staging base
ISO	International Organization for Standardization
IVCSS	internal voice communication switching system

J

J-3	Operations Directorate of a joint staff
J-4	Logistics Directorate of a Joint Staff
JA	Japan
JAOC	joint air operations center
JASC	Joint Actions Steering Committee
JATC	joint air traffic control
JCACC	Joint Combat Airspace Command and Control Course (Army)
JCS	Joint Chiefs of Staff
JFACC	joint force air component commander
JFC	joint force commander
JFCC	Joint Firepower Control Course (USA)
JMCIS	Joint Maritime Command Information System
JOA	joint operations area
JOC	joint operation commander
JPALS	joint precision approach and landing system
JRCC	joint rescue coordination center
JSOAC	joint special operations air component
JSRC	joint search and rescue center
JSTE	joint service training exercise
JTF	joint task force
JTTP	joint tactics, techniques, and procedures
JWG	joint working group

K

kHz	kilohertz
KM	kilometer
KOR	Korea
KY	Kentucky

L

LAAD	local area air defense, low altitude air defense (USMC)
LAMPS	Light Airborne Multipurpose System
lat	latitude
LAWC	local airwarfare commander (USN)
LEC	LAMPS element coordinator
LHA	general purpose amphibious assault ship
LHD	multipurpose amphibious assault ships (with internal dock)
LID	light infantry division
LLTR	low-level transit routes
LMR	land mobile radio
LNO	liaison officer

LOC	location
long	longitude
LOS	line of sight
LPD	amphibious transport dock
LPH	amphibious assault ship, landing platform helicopter
LRIP	low rate initial production
LRS	long range surveillance
LSB	lower side band
LSD	landing ship dock
LTD	laser target designator
LVS	Logistic Vehicle System
LZ	landing zone
LZSO	landing zone support officer

M

MA	Massachusettes
MACCS	Marine Air Command and Control System
MACG	Marine Air Control Group
MACOM	major Army command
MACS	Marine air control squadron
MAGTF	Marine air-ground task force
MAJCOM	major command (USAF)
MANPRINT	Manpower and Personnel Integration Program (USA)
MARFOR	Marine Corps forces
MARLO	Marine liaison officer
MATC	Marine air traffic control
MATCALS	Marine Air Traffic Control and Landing System
MATCD	Marine air traffic control detachment
MAW	Marine aircraft wing
MCAS	Marine Corps Air Station
MCB	Marine Corps Base
MCCDC	Marine Corps Combat Development Command
MCS	maneuver control system
MCWP	Marine Corps Warfare Publication
MD	Maryland
mech	mechanized
MEDEVAC	aeromedical evacuation
MEF	Marine expeditionary force
METT-T	mission, enemy, terrain, and weather, troops and support available, time available
MEU	Marine expeditionary unit
MEU (SOC)	Marine expeditionary unit (special operations capable)
MFC	multinational force commander
MHE	materials handling equipment
MI	military intelligence
mi	mile
MILSTRIP	Military Standard Requisitioning and Issue Procedure
min	minute
MLS	microwave landing system
MMLS	Mobile Microwave Landing System

MMT	Marine air traffic control mobile team
MN	Minnesota
MOA	memorandum of agreement
MOB	main operations base
MOG	maximum (aircraft) on the ground
MOOTW	military operations other than war
MOPP	mission-oriented protective posture
MOS	military occupational specialty
MOTS	Mobile Tower System
mph	miles per hour
MRAALS	Marine Remote Area Approach and Landing System
MRC	major regional contingency
MRR	minimum-risk route
MRSP	mobility readiness spares package
MS	Mississippi
MSE	mobile subscriber equipment
MSL	mean sea level
MTTP	multiservice tactics, techniques, and procedures

N

NAB	Naval Amphibious Base
NAF	numbered Air Forces
NALE	naval and amphibious liaison element
NAS	naval air station; national airspace system
NATTC	Naval Air Technical Training Center
NATO	North Atlantic Treaty Organization
NAV	navigational
NAVAIDS	navigational aids
NAVAIR	Naval Air Systems Command
NAVFOR	Navy forces
NAVSOP	Navy Standing Operating Procedures
NBC	nuclear, biological, and chemical
NC	North Carolina
NCA	National Command Authorities
NCO	noncommissioned officer
NCOIC	noncommissioned officer in charge
NDB	nondirectional beacon
NDC	Naval Doctrine Command
NEA	Northeast Asia
NEF	naval expeditionary force
NEO	noncombatant evacuation operation
NFA	no-fire area; no fuels area
NG	National Guard
NGF	naval gunfire
NH	New Hampshire
NIL	little or none (in reference to breaking action)
NLOS	nonline of sight
NLT	not later than
NM	nautical miles
NOE	nap of the earth

NOTAM	notice to airmen
NTACS	Navy tactical air control system
NVD	night vision device
NVG	night vision goggles
NY	New York

O

O1	Second Lieutenant (USA/USAF/USMC)/Ensign (USN)
O2	First Lieutenant (USA/USAF/USMC)/Lieutenant (j.g.) (USN)
O3	Captain (USA/USAF/USMC)/Lieutenant (USN)
O4	Major (USA/USAF/USMC)/Lieutenant Commander (USN)
O5	Lieutenant Colonel (USA/USAF/USMC)/Commander (USN)
OAC	Officer Advance Course (USA)
OBC	Officer Basic Course (USA)
OCONUS	outside the continental United States
OCU	orderwire control unit
OIC	officer in charge
OJT	on-the-job-training
OK	Oklahoma
OPCON	operational control
OPLAN	operation plan
OPNAVINST	Chief of Naval Operations Instruction
OPORD	operation order
OPR	office of primary responsibility
ops	operations
OPTASK	operational task
OR	Oregon
ORD	operational requirements document
OS	operations specialist; operating system
OTC	officer in tactical command (USN)
ovhd	overhead
ovrn	over run

P

PA	Pennsylvania
PACAF	Pacific Air Forces
PAR	precision approach radar
PBX	private branch exchange
PCC	Pre-command Course (USA)
PCG	Position Certification Guide (USAF)
PCN	pavement classification number
PDS	processor display system
PDS	power distribution system
PHIBRON	amphibious squadron
PIRAZ	positive identification radar advisory zone
PIREP	pilot report
PJ	individual pararescue specialist; project code
PLS	personal locator system
PLS	palletized loading system

POL	petroleum, oils, and lubricants
PR	personnel recovery
PSRC	Presidential selective Reserve call-up
PSS	plans and support section
pwr	power
PZ	pickup zone

Q

QA	quality assurance

R

R&S	reconnaissance and surveillance
RAM	reliability, availability, and maintainability
RAPCON	radar approach control
RC	Reserve Component
RCL	reception committee lighting
RCP	Runway Crossing Points
rcvr	receiver
REC	radio electronic combat
RESCAP	rescue combat air patrol
ref	reference
req	required
RF	radio frequency
RFC	radar final control
RGR	rapid ground refueling
RLST	remote landing site tower
ROC	required operational capabilities
ROE	rules of engagement
ROZ	restricted operations zone
RRP	rapid refueling point
RST	regional survey team
RTB	return to base
rwy	runway
rx	receive

S

SAAWC	sector antiair warfare coordinator (USMC)
SAC	supporting arms coordinator
SACC	supporting arms coordination center (USN)
SAR	search and rescue
SATCOM	satellite communications
SAWC	sector airwarfare commander (USN); sector air warfare coordinator (USMC)
SB	side band
SC	South Carolina
SEI	special experience identifier (USAF)
SFC	surface
SGT	sergeant

SINCGARS	Single-channel Ground and Airborne Radio System
SLRP	survey, liaison, and reconnaissance party
SNCOIC	senior noncommissioned officer in charge
SOC	special operations command
SOF	special operations force
SOG	special operations group
SOLE	special operations liaison element
SOP	standing operating procedures
SOW	Special Operations Wing
SPINS	special instructions
SPMAGTF	special purpose MAGTF (USMC)
SR	sunrise; special reconnaissance
srce	source
SS	sunset
SSB	single side band
ST	special tactics
STG	special tactics group
STP	system training plan
STS	special tactics squadron
STT	special tactics team
STTL	special tactics team leader
STW	strike warfare
sup	supervise
SUW	surface warfare
SWA	Southwest Asia

T

TAB	tactical air base
TAC	terminal access controller, tactical air commander (USN)
tac	tactical
TAC(A)	tactical air controller
TAC SUP	tactical air support coordinator supervisor
TACAN	tactical air navigation
TACC	tactical air command center (USMC); tactical air control center (USN); tanker/airlift control center (USAF)
TACGRU	tactical air control group
TACON	tactical control
TACOPDAT	tactical operational data
TACP	theater air control party
TACRON	tactical air control squadron
TACS	Theater Air Control System
TACT	tactical aviation control team
TAD	tactical air director
TADC	tactical air direction center (USN)
TADIL	tactical digital information link
TAGS	Theater Air/Ground System
TAIS	Tactical Airspace Integration System
TALCE	tanker airlift control element
TAO	tactical actions officer
TAOC	tactical air operations center (USMC)

TATC	tactical air traffic controller
TB	technical bulletins
TCA	terminal control area
TCG	Task Certification Guide (USAF)
TD	transmitter distributor
TERPES	Tactical Electronic Reconnaissance Processing and Evaluation System
TERPS	terminal instrument procedures
TLZ	tactical landing zone
TM	training manual
tm	team
TN	Tennessee
TOC	tactical operations center
TOE	table of organization and equipment
TPFDD	time-phased force and deployment data
TRADOC	Training and Doctrine Command (USA)
TRAP	tactical recovery of aircraft and personnel
trl	trailer
trnsmtr	transmitter
TRV	tower restoral vehicle
TTCS	tactical terminal control system
TTP	tactics, techniques, and procedures
twr	tower
TX	transmit; Texas
txwy	taxiway

U

UAV	unmanned aerial vehicle
UHF	ultra high frequency
UIC	unit identification code (USA)
unk	unknown
US	United States
USA	United States Army
USAAVNC	United States Army Aviation Center
USACOM	United States Atlantic Command
USAF	United States Air Force
USAFAGOS	United States Air Force Air Ground Operations School
USAFE	United States Air Forces, Europe
USAREUR	United States Army Forces, United States European Command
USB	upper side band
USCENTCOM	United States Central Command
USEUCOM	United States European Command
USFK	United Stated Forces, Korea
USMC	United States Marine Corps
USN	United States Navy
USOUTHCOM	United States Southern Command
USPACOM	United States Pacific Command
USSOCOM	United States Special Operations Command
USSPACECOM	United States Space Command
USSTRATCOM	United States Strategic Command
USTRANSCOM	United States Transportation Command

USW	under sea warfare
UTC	unit type code (USAF)

V

V/STOL	vertical/short takeoff and landing aircraft
VAL	visiting aircraft line
VASI	virtual approach slope indicator
VA	Virginia
VFR	visual flight rules
VHF	very high frequency
VIDS	visual information display system
VIP	very important person
VMC	visual meteorological conditions
VOR	very high frequency omnidirectional range station
VORTAC	VHF omnidirectional range station/tactical air navigation
vsby	visibility

W

WA	Washington
WESTPAC	Western Pacific
wg	wing
WIC-P	wing initial communications package
WOC	wing operations center
WX	weather
WY	Wyoming

X

X-FLOT	cross forward line of own troops

Z

Z	zulu
ZM	Z marker (VHF station location marker)

PART II – TERMS AND DEFINITIONS

Army airspace command and control (A2C2). The Army's application of airspace control to coordinate airspace users for concurrent employment in the accomplishment of assigned missions. (FM 101-5-1/MCRP 5-2A)

Army Air-Ground System (AAGS). The Army system which provides for interface between Army and tactical air support agencies of other Services in the planning, evaluating, processing, and coordinating of air support requirements and operations. It is composed of appropriate staff members, including G-2 air and G-3 air personnel, and necessary communications equipment. (Joint Pub 1-02)

airspace control authority (ACA). The commander designated to assume overall responsibility for the operation of the airspace control system in the airspace control area. (Joint Pub 1-02)

airspace control order (ACO). An order implementing the airspace control plan that provides the details of the approved requests for airspace control measures. It is published either as part of the air tasking order or as a separate document. (Joint Pub 1-02)

airspace control plan (ACP). The document approved by the joint force commander that provides specific planning guidance and procedures for the airspace control system for the joint force area of responsibility/joint operations area. (Joint Pub 1-02)

airspace information center (AIC). The ATS facility that performs the primary A2C2 Services mission and the secondary airspace information services mission.

air operations center (AOC). The principal air operations installation from which aircraft and air warning functions of combat air operations are directed, controlled, and executed. It is the senior agency of the Air Force component commander from which command and control of air operations are coordinated with other components and Services. (Joint Pub 1-02)

air tasking order (ATO). A method used to task and disseminate to components, subordinate units, and command and control agencies projected sorties/capabilities/ forces to targets and specific missions. Normally provides specific instructions to include call signs, targets, controlling agencies, etc., as well as general instructions. (Joint Pub 1-02)

Air Traffic Control and Landing Systems (ATCALSs). Department of Defense facilities, personnel, and equipment (fixed, mobile, and seaborne) with associated avionics to provide safe, orderly, and expeditious aerospace vehicle movements worldwide. (Joint Pub 1-02)

air traffic control center. A unit combining the functions of an area control center and a flight information center. (Joint Pub 1-02)

air traffic control clearance. Authorization by an air traffic control authority for an aircraft to proceed under specified conditions. (Joint Pub 1-02)

air traffic control facility. Any of the component airspace control facilities primarily responsible for providing air traffic control services and, as required, limited tactical control services. (Joint Pub 1-02)

air traffic controller. An air controller especially trained for and assigned to the duty of airspace management and traffic control of airborne objects. (Joint Pub 1-02)

air traffic control service. A service provided for the purpose of: a. preventing collisions: (1) between aircraft; and (2) on the maneuvering area between aircraft and obstructions; and b. expediting and maintaining an orderly flow of air traffic. (Joint Pub 1-02)

air traffic services (ATSs). Air traffic services are defined as those services performed by air traffic control specialist or air traffic control organizations across the range of military operations. These include, but are not limited to, Army airspace command and control (A2C2) services, airspace information services, terminal services, forward area support services, landing area/airfield services, navigational aid services, and air traffic control maintenance services.

battlefield coordination detachment (BCD). An Army liaison provided by the Army component commander to the air operations center (AOC) and/or to the component designated by the joint force commander to plan, coordinate, and deconflict air operations. The battlefield coordination detachment processes Army requests for tactical air support, monitors and interprets the land battle situation for the AOC, and provides the necessary interface for exchange of current intelligence and operaional data. (Joint Pub 1-02)

coordinating altitude (level). A procedural airspace control method to separate fixed- and rotary-wing aircraft by determining an altitude below which fixed-wing aircraft will normally not fly and above which rotary-wing aircraft normally will not fly. The coordinating altitude is normally specified in the airspace control plan and may include a buffer zone for small altitude deviations. (Joint Pub 1-02)

control and reporting center (CRC). A mobile command, control, and communications radar element of the US Air Force theater air control system subordinate to the air operations center. The control and reporting center posesses four modular control equipment operations modules and integrates a comprehensive air picture via multiple data links from air-, sea-, and land-based sensors as well as from its surveillance and control radars. It performs decentralized command and control of joint operations by conducting threat warning, battle management, theater missile defense, weapons control, combat identification, and strategic communications. (Joint Pub 1-02)

control and reporting element (CRE). A mobile radar element of the TACS and is subordinate to the CRC. It is normally deployed into forward areas to extend radar coverage and to provide control of air operations, early warning surveillance, and gap filler service. (USAF)

Dynamic Airspace Management System (DAMS). An automated airspace management computer software program providing a data and graphics display of airspace control measures, handle airspace requests, help resolve airspace conflicts, and helps in the planning of airspace. Used in the AOC during DESERT STORM.

Deployment Phases

a. **Initial Deployment.** Initial deployment begins with securing and establishing an airdrome to receive aircraft using small, lightweight communications and marking equipment. Initial services will include visual flight rules ATC services up to limited instrument flight rules services using man-portable NAVAIDS equipment (for example, TRN-41 TACAN)

b. **Transition Deployment.** Transition deployment begins within 5 to 15 days with the arrival of ATCALS packages that provide the communications capability necessary to interface and or establish a capability to support squadron flying operations. The package augments initial communications packages to expand the capability to operate bare base until permanent communications are installed.

c. **Sustaining Deployment.** Sustaining deployment requires ATCALS packages that provide required IFR capability up to and including dual runway precision approach capability. These packages also ensure a stable theater ATC system to support wing flying operations.

flight coordination center (FCC). A primary Army air traffic control agency that is subordinate to the flight operations center (FOC). It provides flight following as well as information on air traffic movement within its assigned area; monitors Army aircraft operations and provides hostile activity warnings to Army aviation units operating in the airspace; passes instrument flight rules flight plans to the airspace management center for approval and visual flight rules flight plans to the appropriate air traffic services facility; establishes liaison with the air defense command post; and provides communications link between terminal facilities of existing airfields, other nearby airfields, division command posts, other FCCs, and the FOC when the FCC locates in a division area. (FM 101-5-1)

flight operations center (FOC). The element of the tactical Army air traffic regulation system which provides for aircraft flight following, separation of aircraft under instrument conditions, and identification of friendly aircraft to friendly air defense agencies. (Joint Pub 1-02)

joint search and rescue center (JSRC). A primary search and rescue facility suitably staffed by supervisory personnel and equipped for planning, coordinating, and executing joint search and rescue and combat search and rescue operations within the geographical area assigned to the joint force. The facility is operated jointly by personnel from two or more Service or functional components or it may have a multinational staff of personnel from two or more allied or coalition nations (multinational search and rescue center). The joint search and rescue center should be staffed equitably by trained personnel drawn from each joint force component, including US Coast Guard participation where practical. (Joint Pub 1-02)

low level transit routes (LLTR). A temporary corridor of defined dimensions established in the forward area to minimize the risk to friendly aircraft from friendly air defenses or surface forces. (Joint Pub 1-02)

Mobile Microwave Landing System (MMLS). A new USAF system for landing sites/airfields to land USAF airlift assets. Also in the Marine Corps inventory.

Mobile Tower System (MOTS). A vehicular mounted tower with the voice/data digitized communications packages, which replaces the TSQ-70 and the TSW-7A for landing sites/airfields.

minimum-risk route (MRR). A temporary corridor of defined dimensions recommended for use by high-speed, fixed-wing aircraft that presents the minimum known hazards to low-flying aircraft transiting the combat zone. (Joint Pub 1-02)

Precision/Non-precision Recovery System. A precision recovery system is an instrument approach that provides glideslope information to the pilot of an aircraft. A nonprecision recovery system is an instrument approach that does not provide glideslope information to the pilot of an aircraft.

Theater Air-Ground System (TAGS). A system of systems consisting of the Theater Air Control System (TACS) (USAF), the Army Air Ground System (AAGS) (USA), the Marine Air Command and Control System (MACCS) (USMC), and the Navy Tactical Air Control System (Navy TACS) (USN).

INDEX

FM 100-104
MCRP 3-25A
NWP 3-56.3
AFTTP(I) 3-2.23
25 JANUARY 1999

By Order of the Secretary of the Army:

DENNIS J. REIMER
General, United States Army
Chief of Staff

Official:

JOEL B. HUDSON
Administrative Assistant to the
Secretary of the Army
05582

DISTRIBUTION:

Active Army, Army National Guard, and U.S. Army Reserve: To be distributed in accordance with the initial distribution number 115756, requirements for FM 100-104.

☆U.S. GOVERNMENT PRINTING OFFICE:2000-517-714/94636